KRISTEN PARKER

Veins of Ice, Blood of Fire

Copyright © 2025 by Kristen Parker

All rights reserved. No part of this publication may be reproduced, stored or transmitted in any form or by any means, electronic, mechanical, photocopying, recording, scanning, or otherwise without written permission from the publisher. It is illegal to copy this book, post it to a website, or distribute it by any other means without permission.

This novel is entirely a work of fiction. The names, characters and incidents portrayed in it are the work of the author's imagination. Any resemblance to actual persons, living or dead, events or localities is entirely coincidental.

Kristen Parker asserts the moral right to be identified as the author of this work.

Kristen Parker has no responsibility for the persistence or accuracy of URLs for external or third-party Internet Websites referred to in this publication and does not guarantee that any content on such Websites is, or will remain, accurate or appropriate.

Designations used by companies to distinguish their products are often claimed as trademarks. All brand names and product names used in this book and on its cover are trade names, service marks, trademarks and registered trademarks of their respective owners. The publishers and the book are not associated with any product or vendor mentioned in this book. None of the companies referenced within the book have endorsed the book.

First edition

This book was professionally typeset on Reedsy.
Find out more at reedsy.com

Contents

One

The Meeting of Fire and Ice

The night was thick with tension, the air crackling with a cold that seemed to seep deep into the bones of those gathered in the grand hall. The towering spires of the castle gleamed under the moonlight, casting long, angular shadows across the floor. Aeryn stood at the heart of the great chamber, her presence as commanding as the flames she controlled, though her heart felt like the icy winds of her enemies. The Fireborn princess, the daughter of the Flame King, had never quite felt at home within these walls of ice. Yet here she was, on the eve of an event meant to shape the future of the fractured kingdoms. Her people had been invited to the Iceborn capital, a rare and dangerous gesture. There was no room for error.

The atmosphere was heavy, a strange mix of suspicion and anticipation. As Aeryn surveyed the crowd, her sharp violet eyes flicked from one face to another, each one carved from the same stoic, cold demeanor that characterized the Iceborn. Dressed in her fiery crimson gown, she was an outcast among them, a vivid reminder of the conflict that had plagued their lands for centuries.

The clinking of glasses, soft murmurs, and the sharp scent of chilled wine filled the space, but despite the festive appearance, no one truly felt at ease. This was no celebration—this was a diplomatic game, a delicate dance where any misstep could ignite a war.

The Fireborn had never trusted the Iceborn, nor the other way around. Yet both kingdoms knew the importance of this gathering. The Iceborn king, Ivoris, had invited them in an attempt to broker a fragile peace, hoping to solidify alliances that could protect both kingdoms from the looming threats of darkness that had begun to creep from the borders. But Aeryn, with her father's fiery will burning in her heart, was not easily swayed. She stood with arms crossed, her mind calculating every movement, every word spoken, and every glance exchanged.

Then, as if drawn by the pull of fate, her gaze landed on him. Thorne.

The Iceborn warrior, whose name had been whispered with both reverence and fear. Tall, imposing, with silver-blond hair that seemed to shimmer under the flickering light of the torches. His eyes, pale and sharp, flicked toward her as if sensing her stare from across the room. He stood at the far end of the hall, his posture regal, yet there was an air of tension that followed him wherever he went. Aeryn had heard of him before—his reputation was as cold as the icy plains of his homeland. Unyielding. Unforgiving. And now, he was watching her with an intensity that made her pulse quicken.

Their gazes locked for a heartbeat that stretched far too long.

Aeryn's stomach twisted, a flare of warmth igniting in her chest, but she quickly smothered it, forcing the flames to cool within her. She was not here to be distracted by the dangerous allure of the Iceborn. She had a mission—her people depended on her. Yet, despite her resolve, she could not tear her eyes away from him. There was something magnetic about his presence, an unspoken connection that felt like the crackle of fire meeting ice. A delicate, precarious balance.

Before she could look away, the sudden clash of metal rang through the air.

The sound of a blade slicing through the atmosphere—a swift, deadly stroke—shattered the fragile peace of the room.

Aeryn's heart skipped as she instinctively reached for the hilt of the dagger hidden beneath her gown. Her fingers brushed the cold steel, ready to draw it in an instant. The room erupted into chaos. Shouts filled the air, and the air itself seemed to freeze, thickening with a heavy presence that made the flames inside Aeryn grow wild.

Thorne was already moving, his body a blur of controlled precision as he sprinted toward the source of the attack. Aeryn's instincts kicked in. Without thinking, she followed, her heart hammering in her chest as she fought the surge of fire threatening to consume her. She had to stay in control. This was not the time to lose herself to the power that thrummed through her veins.

The assassin struck again, a dark figure cloaked in black, their movements swift and deadly. They lunged toward King Ivoris, his back to them, unsuspecting. Aeryn's eyes narrowed. Without a second thought, she hurled herself into the fray, her fire swirling around her like a protective shield, lighting the room in a burst of vivid flames. The figure recoiled, momentarily blinded by the heat. She could hear their ragged breaths as they tried to escape, but Aeryn was already upon them.

Before she could strike, a sharp, cold force shot through the air, freezing the assassin's limbs in place. Aeryn stopped mid-strike, her fire flickering in surprise.

Thorne stood beside her, his hand outstretched, the air around him thick with ice. His gaze was steady, calculating, but there was a flicker of something else—something she couldn't quite place. He didn't need to speak for her to understand that his icy magic had immobilized the assassin. It was done. The threat was neutralized.

For a long moment, Aeryn stood there, her fire flickering in her hands as she watched him. His cool, unwavering demeanor matched the coldness of his powers. The contrast between them was undeniable, but something within her stirred. She had never been one to rely on anyone, let alone an Iceborn warrior, but the realization hit her with the force of a lightning strike: they were bound together in this moment, whether she wanted it or not.

A low growl rumbled from the assassin as they twisted in the ice, their limbs still frozen. Thorne moved toward them, his footsteps silent against the cold stone floor. Aeryn followed, her instincts pushing her to stay alert. She had no idea who the assassin was or who they worked for, but there was one thing she knew for certain—their attempt had been no ordinary attack. This was orchestrated, planned, and it involved far more than just a simple assassination.

Thorne knelt beside the assassin, his gaze cold, calculating. "Who sent you?" he demanded, his voice as frosty as the winds outside.

The assassin's lips curled into a sneer. "You think I'll talk? You think you can break me with your ice?" they spat, their words laced with venom.

Aeryn felt the heat in her chest flare, the fire threatening to burst from her, but she held it back. She had learned long ago that rage only clouded judgment. Thorne, however, didn't hesitate. His eyes narrowed, and with a swift motion, he raised his hand. The ice around the assassin tightened, sending a jolt of cold through their body. The assassin's breath hitched, and for a moment, Aeryn saw something shift in their eyes—a flash of fear.

"Tell us who you work for, or your suffering will be endless," Thorne's voice was soft, yet there was a chilling finality to it.

The assassin trembled, their resolve cracking. With a final, defiant glare, they hissed, "The Fireborn traitors… They wish to see both kingdoms burn."

Aeryn felt her stomach lurch. Fireborn traitors? The words didn't make sense. No one had dared to speak against the Flame King, not in so long. But this was no simple betrayal—it was a message. Whoever had orchestrated this assassination had set the stage for something much larger, something far more dangerous.

Before Aeryn could respond, the assassin collapsed into unconsciousness, their body sinking into the ice, the cold consuming them entirely. Thorne rose to his feet, his eyes locking onto hers. The air between them was charged, a dangerous mixture of fire and ice that neither could fully control. The silence stretched long, heavy with unspoken words.

"This is just the beginning," Thorne said quietly, his eyes

never leaving hers. "They won't stop."

Aeryn nodded, her hand still resting on the hilt of her dagger. "Then we'll stop them."

As the room began to settle, Aeryn and Thorne stood side by side, the weight of the moment pressing down on them. For the first time, Aeryn understood the depth of the tension between them. It was more than just hatred between their peoples. It was fate. Their worlds were destined to clash, and yet, in this moment, they were united by a common cause. But the question lingered in the back of her mind, as it always did: could they trust each other enough to survive what was coming?

The night was far from over, and the game had just begun.

The embers of her fire flickered low, but Aeryn knew the worst was yet to come.

The hall, once full of laughter and chatter, had now fallen into an uneasy silence, broken only by the soft echo of footsteps as the guards cleared the body of the assassin. The icy air seemed colder now, carrying with it a palpable sense of danger that hung heavy on every breath. Aeryn stood at the center of the room, her fire now dim, but the heat still simmering just beneath her skin. Thorne, silent as ever, remained at her side, his gaze never wavering from the path ahead. He hadn't moved away from her, and she couldn't bring herself to look away either.

The weight of their shared moment hung between them like a thread pulled taut. She could feel the electric tension swirling in the air around them, a dangerous force neither of them could deny. Yet, beneath it, there was something else— something deep and unspoken, a pull that she wasn't sure she was ready to confront.

For a moment, it seemed as if they were the only two people left in the world.

But that silence was shattered by the voice of King Ivoris, harsh and commanding, cutting through the chaos like a blade. "Princess Aeryn, Warrior Thorne," his tone held an edge, but it was unmistakably laced with grudging respect. "I suggest we take this conversation somewhere more… private."

His words were not a request.

Aeryn nodded stiffly, not trusting herself to speak. Her thoughts were still racing, trying to make sense of the assassin's final words. **Fireborn traitors.** It felt impossible to believe, yet the reality of their sudden, coordinated attack was undeniable. Something darker was afoot.

Thorne's sharp eyes met hers, and for the briefest of moments, a silent understanding passed between them. They were being led, but there was no choice. Not now. Not with everything on the line.

The guards moved aside as Ivoris gestured toward a narrow staircase at the far end of the hall. They ascended the stairs in silence, the click of Aeryn's heels and the soft crunch of Thorne's boots on the frost-covered stone echoing in the dimly lit corridor.

They reached a small, private chamber at the top of the tower—a room that seemed far removed from the grand hall, its windows offering a sweeping view of the frozen city below. The wind howled outside, the night's cold pressing against the stone, as if nature itself was trying to break in. Inside, the room was warm, with a fire crackling in the hearth and plush velvet chairs arranged around a low table.

Ivoris gestured toward one of the chairs but did not sit. He stood by the window, his back to them, staring out at the snowy expanse that stretched endlessly beyond the castle walls. "You've both proven yourselves," he said, his voice cold and deliberate. "But we cannot afford to waste any more time with pleasantries. I need answers."

Aeryn crossed her arms, her gaze hardening as she stood with her back to the fire. "Answers? The assassin was one of our own. Who else needs to be told?"

The king turned, his pale blue eyes narrowing. "I need to know where your loyalties truly lie, Princess. Because I cannot risk trusting the Fireborn entirely, not after this."

His words stung, but Aeryn kept her expression unreadable. "My loyalty lies with my people, as it always has."

"You do not speak for your people." Ivoris's voice was low, a warning. "You speak for your father, the Flame King, who is known to be… unstable. I have reason to believe that a faction within your own kingdom is working against both of us."

Aeryn bristled at the insinuation. "Are you suggesting that my father's people are responsible for this attack? That's preposterous."

Ivoris's lip curled slightly, the faintest of smirks playing at the edge of his mouth. "Not your father, no. But I have seen signs. The fire—the rage that runs deep in your veins. There are others who share that… fervor. A dangerous few who think peace is impossible."

Aeryn's mind raced. She had always known that her father's reign was one marked by violence and rage, but she never thought it would lead to this kind of betrayal. She had been raised to believe in her kingdom's strength, but the cracks were starting to show, even in her own heart.

"Then we have a common enemy," Thorne said, his voice

cold, but there was a note of something else in his words—something almost… resigned. He stepped forward, his eyes meeting Aeryn's for the first time in what felt like hours. "We both know that whatever this is, it has nothing to do with us personally. But we'll need to work together if we want to get to the bottom of it."

Aeryn stared at him, her chest tightening. Their shared mission—though logical—felt like a chain being wrapped tighter and tighter around her heart. She had always been taught to distrust the Iceborn, to keep them at arm's length. And yet, here she was, forced into an alliance with one. A warrior who exuded the coldness of winter itself, whose every movement was calculated, precise, like a weapon in waiting.

But the way he looked at her—his gaze unwavering, his jaw tight with determination—it was clear that he too saw the gravity of the situation. And that perhaps, for the first time, their fates were truly intertwined.

"You both are right," Ivoris continued, pulling their attention back to him. "This is bigger than any of us. There are whispers in the east—rumors of a coalition of traitors, both from Fireborn and Iceborn ranks, aiming to shatter the balance. They believe that only through destruction will the kingdoms ever know peace."

Aeryn's heart sank. The cold weight of the king's words settled over her like a thick fog. "And you think we can stop them?"

"I don't think we have a choice," Ivoris replied, his voice now strangely softer. "The fire inside you, Princess… It may be the only thing that can match the ice they are bringing."

Aeryn glanced at Thorne, who stood rigid, his expression unreadable. He was as cold as the winter itself, but there was a flicker of something—something that resembled… fear? Or was it doubt?

"We can't be the only ones who are capable of stopping them," she said, her voice low, almost to herself. "We need to know who's pulling the strings."

"That is why I'm putting you both together," Ivoris said, his eyes hardening again. "I trust no one else."

Aeryn's blood ran cold. The implications of his words were clear. She and Thorne, enemies in the eyes of their people, now had no choice but to work together. To track down the traitors, to uncover the conspiracy that had wormed its way into the very heart of both kingdoms.

"Is that your final word, King Ivoris?" Thorne's voice cut through the air like a blade, his gaze unwavering.

The king nodded, a glint of cold satisfaction in his eyes. "Yes. Your alliance is the only chance we have. If you fail, we all fall."

The silence in the room was thick with unspoken tension, the weight of their fate now resting on their shoulders. Aeryn and Thorne exchanged one final glance, the spark of something—uncertainty, desire, and perhaps the beginning of trust—passing between them.

They had no choice now but to face the storm together.

Aeryn stepped forward, her fire reigniting within her. She would not fail. She couldn't.

"Then let's get to work."

And with that, the game had truly begun.

Two

Fates Entangled

The night air was so cold it bit at her skin like shards of glass. Aeryn's breath fogged the air before her, twisting in the icy wind that howled through the narrow streets of the Iceborn capital. The world seemed to shrink around her, her feet crunching against the snow-covered ground, the only sound in the desolate alleyways the beating of her heart. Her hand hovered over the dagger at her waist, ready for whatever threat might come next. The sharp scent of frost hung thick in the air, the chill of it seeping into her very bones.

Behind her, Thorne moved like a shadow—silent, composed, and far too composed for Aeryn's liking. She could feel him more than she could see him, his presence like a weight pressing on her back. She didn't trust him, not yet. But she couldn't deny the unspoken bond between them that had been formed when they had fought together, side by side, in the grand hall. It was impossible to ignore.

"Keep moving," Thorne said, his voice low but commanding. His footsteps made no sound in the snow as he matched her stride, his gaze scanning the dark corners of the narrow street. His presence was like ice itself—unyielding, cold, and yet there was something else lurking beneath the surface. Aeryn wasn't sure if it was fear or something more dangerous—something that could destroy them both.

The night was dark, lit only by the pale glow of the moon reflecting off the snow that blanketed the kingdom. The city around them was quiet, unnaturally so. Aeryn had never known the Iceborn capital to be so still, and she couldn't shake the feeling that they were being hunted. Every shadow, every gust of wind seemed to whisper warnings in her ears.

"Do you think they'll come after us?" Aeryn asked, her voice barely above a whisper, though the words felt heavy in her mouth.

Thorne didn't look at her, his eyes locked on the path ahead. "They already have."

Aeryn's chest tightened, the weight of his words settling in. She had expected the assassination attempt to have been part of some larger plot, but to hear him say it so matter-of-factly only made the danger feel more real. They were not just being pursued—they were being hunted, and with every step, they were growing closer to the heart of whatever conspiracy had been set in motion.

The alleyway opened into a wider square, the moonlight casting long shadows on the stone buildings. Aeryn paused, looking back toward the dark alley they had just emerged from, her senses heightened. Her fingers itched for the comfort of fire, the heat that burned inside her, ready to be unleashed. But there was no time for that now. They needed to keep moving.

"I know where we're going," she said, her voice steady despite the unease that gnawed at her. "I can take us to the old tunnels beneath the city. We'll be safe there."

Thorne nodded, his gaze finally flicking to her. "Lead the way."

Her eyes met his for the first time since they'd fled the castle. There was something in his gaze—something like restraint, as though he were holding something back. Aeryn couldn't place it, but it unsettled her.

They moved swiftly, Aeryn leading them through the winding streets of the city. Her thoughts were racing, but the path ahead was clear. She had been raised on stories of the underground tunnels that ran beneath the Iceborn capital— hidden, forgotten places where few could reach. The Fireborn knew about them, though the Iceborn had long since stopped using them. It would be their safest escape, at least for now.

The walls of the buildings around them grew higher as they moved deeper into the city, the sounds of their footsteps muffled by the thick snow that had fallen throughout the night. The wind howled through the alleys, and Aeryn could feel it biting into her exposed skin. She clenched her jaw against the cold, but it was nothing compared to the fire that smoldered beneath her skin.

Thorne was close, too close. She could feel the pull of him behind her, his presence pressing against her in ways that had nothing to do with the danger they were in. It was an unfamiliar sensation, something she couldn't afford to entertain. But the tension between them, that sharp, magnetic energy, refused to be ignored.

"You're not like the others," she said suddenly, breaking the silence that had grown between them. She didn't know why she said it—perhaps she just needed to fill the quiet, to anchor herself in something she could understand.

Thorne didn't answer immediately, his expression unreadable as he kept pace with her. When he finally spoke, his voice was low, and there was a trace of something almost like amusement in his tone. "And what exactly do you mean by that?"

"You don't act like the other Iceborn," Aeryn clarified. "You don't carry yourself like you're better than everyone else. You're different."

He didn't respond at first, and for a moment, Aeryn wondered if she'd said something wrong. But then he gave a small, almost imperceptible shrug. "Maybe because I'm not like the rest of them."

Aeryn's mind raced, trying to decipher his words. She had never known an Iceborn to admit anything like that. The Iceborn were proud, stoic, and fiercely protective of their kingdom and their place in the world. Thorne's words were unexpected, and for a moment, Aeryn found herself intrigued.

But there was no time for curiosity now. The sound of footsteps ahead, echoing through the streets, pulled her from her thoughts. She froze, her heart pounding in her chest as her hand automatically went to the hilt of her dagger. Thorne's eyes narrowed, and without a word, he moved forward, his steps swift and sure.

Aeryn followed closely behind, the fire within her stirring, waiting to be unleashed. But she kept it controlled—there was no need to draw attention just yet. They were almost there.

As they turned the corner, a shadow darted from one of the side alleys, moving so quickly that Aeryn barely had time to react. She heard Thorne's sharp intake of breath as the figure lunged toward them, a gleaming blade raised high. The assassin's movements were fast, precise, but Aeryn was faster.

She spun to the side, her body coiling with the familiar surge of heat, and in an instant, the fire roared to life in her palms. She thrust her hand forward, sending a wave of flame toward the assassin. The heat was blinding, a searing burst of orange that lit up the street. The assassin was thrown back, their body slamming into the stone wall with a sickening thud.

Aeryn stood there, chest heaving, the fire still flickering around her fingertips. She hadn't meant to unleash so much of her power, but the need to protect Thorne, to survive, had overridden her control. She turned toward him, her breath coming in sharp gasps.

Thorne stood a few paces behind her, his eyes fixed on the fallen assassin, but there was no surprise on his face. Instead, he gave a single, sharp nod. "Nice work."

Aeryn's lips parted in disbelief. "Nice work?" she echoed, her voice rising. "You didn't even—"

"I had it under control," Thorne interrupted, stepping forward with a coldness that stilled the anger in Aeryn's chest. His eyes were still locked on the assassin's lifeless body, his expression unreadable. "We need to move. There's more of them."

Aeryn's pulse quickened, and without another word, she followed him. The fire in her veins still burned hot, but she forced it down. They were not done yet.

The streets ahead were silent, but Aeryn knew that wouldn't last. They were far from safe.

She could feel the weight of their fate pressing down on her, on both of them. She had always known her powers were dangerous, that they would one day lead her down a path she couldn't control. But with Thorne… with him, she felt the tug of something stronger—something that both terrified and fascinated her.

He was the ice to her fire.

And together, they were about to ignite a storm neither of them could predict.

The further they moved into the city's labyrinth, the more tightly entwined their fates became. Neither of them could escape what was coming, no matter how hard they tried to resist it.

The prophecy was already in motion.

And their destinies had already been sealed.

The wind cut through the narrow alleyways like a blade, whistling as it whipped through the tall, ice-coated buildings. The city was a maze of stone and frost, and Aeryn could feel the weight of it pressing in on her. Her heart pounded in her chest, her breath coming out in ragged gasps as she followed Thorne through the twisting streets. Each turn, each shadow that moved in the corner of her eye, felt like an enemy ready to strike. The silence was deafening, the tension thick in the air.

The assassin's body was already gone—swept away by Thorne's icy magic, as if he had never been there at all. Aeryn's heart was still racing, her senses heightened, but there was no time to reflect. They had barely survived this first attack, and she knew more would come. **They're tracking us. They've been watching us from the start.**

Thorne's presence beside her was a constant reminder that they were linked now, not just by the danger but by something else—something far more dangerous. Every step she took seemed to echo between them, their connection growing tighter and tighter. She didn't know if it was the fire inside her that was drawing her to him or something else, but she couldn't deny it. There was something about him—something strange and magnetic.

Aeryn's hand instinctively flexed at her side, and she could feel the heat of her powers, simmering just beneath her skin. But the tension in the air had nothing to do with the cold or the fire—it had everything to do with the connection between her and Thorne.

His voice cut through the silence, low and controlled. "Keep your wits about you. We're almost there."

She glanced at him, catching a glimpse of his profile in the moonlight. His face was set, his jaw clenched in concentration, but there was something else—something almost weary in the lines of his face. She wondered how much of it was from the weight of the world they both carried and how much was from the prophecy that loomed over them like a shadow.

"Where exactly are we going?" she asked, her voice sharp despite herself. She had assumed he knew the way, but after everything that had happened, she needed something to hold on to. Something solid.

"There's a place on the outskirts of the city," he replied, never slowing his pace. "A safehouse. We'll regroup there, figure out what to do next."

"Safehouse?" Aeryn repeated, disbelief curling in her stomach. "And you trust it?"

Thorne's gaze flicked to her briefly, a quick, cold glance that held more than just the practical. "I trust no one. But it's the best chance we have."

The words hung in the air between them, heavy and final.

Aeryn wanted to argue, to say something—anything—but she couldn't find the words. Instead, she focused on the path ahead, pushing her doubts to the back of her mind.

They passed through the deserted streets, moving deeper into the heart of the city, where the icy wind howled louder, biting through the heavy layers of her clothing. The further they went, the more isolated they became, the eerie quiet wrapping itself around them like a shroud. Aeryn's senses were on high alert, every sound, every shift of the air making her flinch.

"Stay close," Thorne said again, his voice barely audible above the wind. His hand rested on the hilt of a blade at his side, his body coiled like a spring, ready to strike at any moment. Aeryn followed closely, her heart racing as they rounded another corner, coming to a long, narrow street lined with ancient stone buildings. Their dark outlines seemed to loom over them, watching, waiting.

And then, it happened.

A sudden crash broke the stillness, followed by the sound of footsteps—heavy, purposeful steps—echoing off the walls. Aeryn froze, her pulse jumping in her throat. Thorne was already moving, his movements quick and fluid. Without a word, he grabbed her arm and pulled her into the shadows of a nearby alcove, pressing her against the cold stone of the building.

Aeryn's breath caught in her throat, her body pressed against his in the darkness. For a moment, the world seemed to stop— her heartbeat racing in her ears, the tension between them thickening. His chest was warm against her, the heat of his body radiating through the layers of their clothing. And yet, there was no time to dwell on it. Not now.

The footsteps grew louder, drawing closer. Aeryn's hand tightened around her dagger, her senses sharp. Thorne's gaze flicked to her, his icy blue eyes cold and calculating. He reached for her hand, guiding it to the side of her dagger, silently telling her to stay calm.

The footsteps stopped just in front of the alcove. Aeryn could feel the presence of the figures outside, their breath visible in the night air. They were close—too close. Her heart was a drumbeat in her chest, and she could feel the fire inside her stirring again, itching to be released. But she resisted, keeping her powers in check.

Thorne shifted slightly, his body pressing closer to hers, if only by a fraction. His whisper came low, barely audible. "Wait for it."

Aeryn barely had time to react when the first figure moved past them, his cloak sweeping just inches away from her face. She held her breath, the moment stretching as if time had slowed. The figure stopped for a heartbeat, his boot scraping against the stone. Then, with a sharp intake of breath, he continued forward, moving deeper into the alley.

Aeryn let out the breath she'd been holding, her body still pressed against Thorne's. But the moment wasn't over. The second figure followed quickly, their steps too light, too quick. The scent of metal and frost filled the air as the figure drew closer.

Thorne tensed, his eyes narrowing, but he didn't make a move. Not yet.

And then, a third figure appeared.

Aeryn's heart skipped a beat.

This one was different. They wore no cloak, no disguise. Their face was exposed—sharp, cruel, and unmistakable.

Aeryn's blood ran cold.

It was a woman.

She stood still for a moment, her dark eyes sweeping over the street, scanning for any sign of movement. Aeryn's pulse thundered in her ears, her hand clenched tightly around her dagger. She had to move. She couldn't stay hidden any longer.

But just as the woman took a step forward, Thorne made his move.

With lightning speed, he darted from the alcove, his hand shooting out to grab the woman by the throat. Her gasp of surprise was short-lived as Thorne spun her around, slamming her into the stone wall. Aeryn's heart pounded in her chest as she rushed to his side, dagger raised, but Thorne held a firm grip on the woman's throat.

"Who sent you?" Thorne demanded, his voice a low, dangerous growl.

The woman's eyes glinted with defiance, but she remained silent, her lips pressed tight. Aeryn stepped forward, her fire flaring briefly, and the heat wrapped itself around her fingertips like a warning. The air around them thickened with tension.

Thorne's gaze met hers for a fraction of a second—silent, questioning. The woman would not break under pressure, but Aeryn knew there was one way to get the answers they needed.

The fire burned hotter inside her, building like a storm, her breath quickening with each passing moment. The woman's defiance would be her undoing. Slowly, she raised her hand, and the flames sparked to life, lighting the street in a burst of warmth.

The woman flinched, her eyes wide. The fire around Aeryn's fingers danced, an extension of her will, scorching the air, but still, the woman said nothing.

Thorne's grip tightened, his voice like ice. "Tell us. Now."

The woman's breath hitched, her eyes darting to the flames before she spoke in a whisper, her voice laced with venom. "You think this is over? You think you're the only ones with power? You're a fool."

Aeryn's heart slammed in her chest. She couldn't afford to hesitate. Not now.

Before she could strike, Thorne's eyes flicked to hers, the unspoken command clear. "Get ready."

In one fluid motion, Thorne released the woman, his hand moving like lightning as he grabbed her by the wrist and twisted, slamming her into the ground with a force that left Aeryn breathless. The woman struggled, but her movements were sluggish, weaker now that her hidden support had been cut off.

Aeryn moved to stand beside him, her dagger raised high, her fire crackling around her fingertips. "Who do you work for?" she demanded once more.

The woman's lips curled into a sneer, blood trickling from her mouth as she spat. "You'll find out soon enough. All of you will burn."

Thorne's face remained cold, but there was a flicker of something darker in his eyes—something that mirrored the fire growing within Aeryn. "We're done here."

With one swift motion, Thorne turned, dragging the woman with him. The danger wasn't over, but for the first time since their escape, Aeryn felt like she might have a chance to find the answers she needed.

But she knew one thing for sure.

They were both trapped now, caught in the storm, and it was

only just beginning.

Three

The Forbidden Bond

The cold was biting, an icy hand gripping at Aeryn's lungs as they trekked further into the wilderness. The world around them had changed as they moved deeper into enemy territory—long stretches of barren land replaced by jagged mountains that seemed to scrape the sky. The wind howled through the peaks, swirling snow and ice in thick, blinding curtains. Yet, despite the landscape's beauty, there was something foreboding about the silence that hung over them. The Earth seemed to hold its breath, as if waiting for something to break.

Aeryn pulled her cloak tighter around her shoulders, trying to stave off the chill, but the cold could never compare to the storm brewing within her. There was a tension in the air, something that crackled between her and Thorne like an electric current. They hadn't spoken much since their escape from the Iceborn capital, each lost in their own thoughts, yet the silence felt heavier with every step they took together. Each time she looked at him, her heart pounded faster, her mind whirling with questions she didn't know how to ask.

Thorne was at her side, his icy presence as cold and unyielding as ever, but there was something different about him now. The fire within her had already drawn her toward him, and despite the distance between them, she could feel his every movement—every glance. The space that separated them seemed to grow more insufferable as they continued their journey.

"You're quiet," Thorne said, his voice low but carrying through the silence.

Aeryn didn't answer immediately, instead focusing on the treacherous path ahead. Their feet crunched over the snow, each step a labor. Her breath billowed in front of her, a cloud of mist in the frozen air. They had been walking for hours, and even though the sun was hidden behind a thick blanket of clouds, the day seemed endless.

"I was thinking," she said finally, her voice barely above a whisper. "About what we learned last night."

Thorne's eyes flicked to her, the frost in his gaze momentarily softening. "The prophecy."

Aeryn nodded, though the words felt heavy in her chest. She could still see the way the ancient scholar had spoken, his voice a tremor of fear as he recited the words from the scroll they had uncovered beneath the Iceborn city. The prophecy had been clear, unyielding in its certainty. **One shall burn with fire, the other shall freeze in ice. One must die, the other live. Only then can peace be restored.**

At the time, Aeryn had dismissed it. Prophecies were just stories—words written by seers who had no idea how the world would truly unfold. But as they walked through the snow, with every step they took deeper into enemy land, the weight of those words grew heavier.

"I don't believe it," she said, forcing the words out with more conviction than she felt. "I won't."

Thorne said nothing at first, his gaze distant as his boots crunched over the snow. They had crossed into the Iceborn kingdom's borders nearly an hour ago, their path leading them farther away from the safety of the cities and into more dangerous territory.

"Do you think we can avoid it?" Thorne asked, his voice quiet. "The prophecy."

Aeryn looked at him sharply, her heart thumping in her chest. He was looking at her now, his expression unreadable, his lips pressed into a firm line. "I'm not afraid of the prophecy," she said, her voice stronger than before. "We can change the future. We make our own path."

Thorne's gaze darkened. "You say that now, but fate has a way of twisting things. We don't control everything."

The words hung in the air, the tension between them thickening with each passing moment. Aeryn's thoughts were swirling, fighting against the certainty of the prophecy. She couldn't allow herself to believe in it. Not now. Not when she was still so uncertain of everything, including the man at her side.

But there was more than just the prophecy. There was the bond that seemed to grow between them every day, something unspoken and undeniable. The fire inside her had become something impossible to ignore whenever Thorne was near. And though his cold, detached nature should have pushed her away, it had only drawn her closer.

"I don't trust it," she said at last, breaking the silence. "This prophecy, this fate... it feels like a trap."

Thorne's lips quirked, a slight, almost imperceptible smile that did nothing to soften his hard gaze. "You don't trust me either."

The bluntness of his words shocked her, and she felt her stomach tighten with something she couldn't quite place. "I didn't say that."

"No," Thorne said, his voice low, "you didn't. But I can see it in your eyes. You're afraid of me. Of what I am."

Aeryn opened her mouth to argue, but the words caught in her throat. She wasn't afraid of him—at least, she didn't think she was. But there was a part of her that trembled whenever she was near him, a flicker of fear mixed with something else, something more dangerous.

"You're right," she said softly, admitting it to herself more than to him. "I don't trust you. Not completely."

Thorne's eyes softened for just a moment, a flicker of something human passing across his cold façade. But it was gone as quickly as it came. "You think I'm the enemy, don't you?"

Aeryn hesitated. It was a difficult question, one she had wrestled with since the moment their paths had crossed. The Iceborn and Fireborn had been enemies for as long as anyone could remember. Their people were bound by hatred, by centuries of bloodshed and mistrust. She had been raised to believe that the Iceborn were her enemies—nothing more, nothing less.

But Thorne... He was different.

Aeryn turned her face away from him, the harsh wind biting at her skin, and looked out across the barren landscape. The mountains towered in the distance, their jagged peaks piercing the stormy sky like the claws of some great beast. The sight sent a shiver down her spine, and for a moment, she wondered if she was walking into the very jaws of that beast.

"I don't know what to think anymore," she admitted, her voice barely above a whisper. "Everything's changed. My world… it's falling apart."

Thorne's eyes were unwavering, and for a moment, Aeryn thought he might say something—some harsh, cutting remark that would push them further apart. But instead, he simply nodded, as though he understood.

"I didn't choose this either," he said quietly. "I didn't choose to be part of this war, but the prophecy… it's something neither of us can escape."

The words hung between them, thick with meaning. Aeryn didn't know whether to take his words as a warning or a promise. The tension between them was palpable now, heavier than the cold that surrounded them. Her heart hammered in her chest, and she couldn't decide whether it was fear or something else.

"I don't want to be a part of this," she said suddenly, her voice stronger than before. "I don't want to be a pawn in some ancient prophecy that says one of us has to die."

Thorne's eyes flashed, a brief spark of something dangerous crossing his features. "Neither do I. But we don't have a choice. Not anymore."

Aeryn's chest tightened at the words. She wanted to deny it, wanted to tell him that they could escape, that they could find a way out of this nightmare. But deep down, she knew he was right. The prophecy was inescapable.

The silence stretched long between them, neither of them

speaking for a long moment. The wind howled, a mournful cry against the frozen landscape, but it felt like the world was holding its breath.

"I won't let you die," Aeryn said finally, her voice trembling despite her best efforts to keep it steady. She didn't know why she said it—perhaps because it was the only thing that made sense in that moment. "I'll find a way to save you."

Thorne's eyes softened again, and for the briefest of moments, he looked almost… human. "And what if it's me who has to save you?"

Aeryn didn't know how to answer. What if it was him? What if the only way to break the prophecy was for one of them to die?

They continued walking in silence, the sound of their footsteps swallowed by the howling wind. As the mountains loomed closer, a sense of inevitability settled over Aeryn. She wasn't sure where this path would lead them, but she knew that the bond between them was only growing stronger with each passing day. The fire inside her, the one that had always burned so brightly, now pulsed with a new intensity whenever Thorne was near.

But what did it mean? What did any of it mean?

They had both been swept into this, and now there was no way out. The prophecy was like a shadow, stretching out before them, and with every step they took, it grew closer. The bond that had begun as something dangerous and forbidden was now something more. It was inescapable.

And Aeryn was beginning to realize just how much she might be willing to sacrifice to survive it.

The mountains loomed larger with each step they took, their

jagged peaks scraping against the slate-gray sky. The path was treacherous, the wind fierce, howling through the cliffs and carrying with it a bitter, biting cold that seemed to gnaw at the very marrow of Aeryn's bones. She kept her head down, her cloak pulled tightly around her body, but no amount of warmth could quell the unease that had settled deep inside her. The prophecy haunted her thoughts, twisting through her mind like the wind itself—unrelenting, inevitable.

Beside her, Thorne moved with the silent grace of someone who had grown up with the mountains, whose steps were sure and measured despite the treacherous terrain. He was a force of nature in his own right—cold, calculating, yet strangely magnetic. Aeryn could feel him beside her, each movement he made seeming to echo in her chest, stirring something deep within her, something she wasn't prepared to face.

"Do you know where we're going?" Aeryn asked, her voice barely rising above the wind's cry. She didn't expect an answer, but she needed something—anything to distract her from the questions spinning in her mind.

Thorne glanced at her, his pale eyes hard and unreadable. "I know the way. There's a settlement on the far side of these mountains. We'll be safe there, for now."

Safe. The word seemed so foreign now. They were in the heart of enemy territory, and safety felt as distant as the sun hidden behind the dark clouds. But Aeryn had learned to trust Thorne in ways she hadn't expected. They were bound by the same fate, by the same prophecy, and no matter how much she fought against it, no matter how much she longed for freedom, she knew that they had no choice but to keep moving forward.

The cold winds howled louder, and Aeryn could feel her body tiring, her limbs aching with every step. Her powers, the fire that burned so fiercely inside her, seemed to weaken against the relentless cold of the Iceborn land. She had always been accustomed to warmth, to the heat of the flames that were her birthright. But here, in the icy grip of the mountains, she felt the fire inside her flickering, struggling to stay alive.

"Are you alright?" Thorne's voice cut through her thoughts, a low, concerned murmur that caught her off guard.

Aeryn blinked, surprised that he had noticed. She hadn't thought him the type to care for anyone's well-being, especially not hers. But there was a sharpness in his eyes, a flicker of something that looked like concern, and for a moment, she wondered if he was more human than he let on.

"I'm fine," she replied quickly, though her voice betrayed her. Her breath came in short, uneven gasps, and the cold was starting to seep into her bones. "Just tired."

Thorne didn't respond immediately, but he slowed his pace just slightly, allowing her to catch up. His presence, like a wall of ice, was both comforting and unnerving. It was strange, this feeling that had developed between them—this connection that neither of them had chosen but both were forced to accept. It was more than just physical attraction. It was something deeper, something that tied them together in ways they both couldn't yet understand.

The silence between them grew as they continued on, the sound of their footsteps muffled by the thick snow beneath their feet. The wind had died down a little, but the atmosphere felt heavier, as if the very air around them was holding its breath.

Aeryn's mind kept returning to the prophecy. **One shall burn with fire, the other shall freeze in ice. One must die, the other live.** The words echoed in her head, a constant reminder of the danger they faced. How could they possibly escape that fate? How could they avoid the inevitable when the world itself seemed to have conspired against them?

"You're thinking about the prophecy again," Thorne said, his voice cutting through the silence.

Aeryn didn't bother denying it. "How could I not? It's all we have now. It's all we're left with."

Thorne's gaze flicked to her, the sharpness of his expression softening just slightly. "We don't have to follow it."

Aeryn raised an eyebrow, surprised by his words. "What do you mean? You heard it just as clearly as I did. One of us has to die. There's no avoiding it."

"I didn't say it would be easy," Thorne said, his voice steady. "But fate isn't a straight path. It's full of choices. And we can make our own."

Aeryn's heart skipped at the conviction in his voice. There was a fire there, a spark that she hadn't noticed before. It was strange to hear it from someone like Thorne—someone who had been raised on the cold, unyielding doctrines of the Iceborn. She had always thought the Iceborn were slaves to their fate, bound by honor and tradition, their lives dictated by a destiny they had no choice but to accept.

But Thorne was different. She could see that now.

"Do you think we can change the prophecy?" Aeryn asked, her voice trembling despite her best efforts to keep it steady. She wasn't sure why she was asking him—why she was letting him into her thoughts so easily. Perhaps it was the journey, or perhaps it was the bond that had formed between them, but she found herself seeking his answer.

Thorne was quiet for a long moment, his eyes fixed on the distant peaks. The wind howled again, but it didn't seem to touch him. The cold was a part of him, just as the fire was a part of her. And somewhere, in the middle of that frozen landscape, their paths had converged.

"I don't know," he said at last, his voice softer now, less certain. "But I'd rather die fighting for a different future than accept the one they've written for us."

Aeryn's heart skipped. She hadn't expected him to say that—hadn't expected him to admit, even to himself, that there was more to their journey than just survival. There was a chance. A chance to defy the prophecy.

Her mind raced. Could they really change their fate? Could they rewrite the future, as Thorne suggested? Or were they just fooling themselves into thinking they had control over something they could never truly escape?

As if reading her thoughts, Thorne looked at her again, his gaze steady and intense. "But if we do this, we do it together. I won't let you carry the weight of this alone."

Aeryn's breath caught in her throat. The sincerity in his voice was impossible to ignore. It was the first time he had said anything that wasn't wrapped in cold, detached indifference. For a moment, she wondered if she had misjudged him, if the man before her was someone entirely different from the warrior she had come to expect.

"I won't let you die," Aeryn said quietly, the words slipping out before she could stop them. The certainty in her voice startled her, but she didn't take it back. "I don't care what the prophecy says. We'll find a way."

Thorne didn't respond immediately, his eyes narrowing as if he were weighing her words. For a brief, flickering moment, she thought he might pull away, might dismiss her words as naive. But instead, he gave a small nod, his lips curling into something that almost resembled a smile.

"Then we'll fight together," he said, his voice low but firm. "And we won't stop until we find a way to change the outcome."

The words hung in the air, a promise that neither of them could break. They were bound by fate, yes, but also by something more—a shared determination to fight against the forces that sought to tear them apart.

Aeryn felt the fire inside her flare in response, the heat rising in her chest. They were in this together. And for the first time in a long time, she felt something she hadn't expected: hope.

They continued walking, the snow crunching beneath their feet, their steps synchronized as they moved toward the unknown. The wind had begun to die down, and a strange stillness settled over the land. The mountains were vast and unforgiving, but they were not alone.

For the first time, Aeryn felt like she wasn't just walking toward the prophecy—she was walking toward a future they could build together.

And no matter how impossible it seemed, no matter how dark the road ahead, she knew they would face it together.

Because that was the only way they could survive.

The wind shifted, carrying the scent of the coming storm.

And Aeryn knew, deep in her bones, that whatever was waiting for them at the end of this path, it would be the fight of their lives.

Four

The First Flame

The night had fallen over the mountains like a heavy cloak, the sky a deep, impenetrable black. Aeryn and Thorne had long since left the relative safety of the open trail, winding their way through thick forest and rocky outcrops. The air around them felt thinner, more suffocating the deeper they ventured into the unknown. Aeryn's breath came in short, shallow bursts, her senses heightened as they moved farther away from the watchful eyes of the Iceborn kingdom.

Their surroundings were eerily quiet, save for the occasional creak of frozen branches swaying in the wind. The night seemed to be holding its breath, and Aeryn could feel the weight of it pressing down on her, settling like a shadow in her chest. The flickering of the fire in her palms, which had always been a constant companion, was now a distant memory, suppressed by the cold that clung to everything here. Her fire felt weak, stifled by the oppressive chill.

Aeryn's footsteps were soft, deliberate, the snow crunching beneath her boots in an unsettling rhythm. Beside her, Thorne moved with the kind of quiet that only the Iceborn were capable of—a silent predator, ready to strike at any moment. His ice-blue eyes scanned the landscape ahead, his posture tense, like a wolf on alert.

"Aeryn," Thorne said, his voice a low murmur in the otherwise still night. "We need to stop."

Aeryn barely heard him at first, the noise of the wind in her ears overwhelming. But his words cut through the stillness, and she glanced at him, her brow furrowing. He was looking toward the treeline, his gaze intense and sharp.

"What is it?" she asked, her hand inching toward the dagger at her side. Her fire had grown restless, the heat within her pushing against the cold, but she couldn't afford to release it—at least not yet.

Thorne didn't answer immediately, but the tightening of his jaw told her all she needed to know. He was listening, waiting for something.

A sound. A shift in the air.

Then, it came. The faintest rustle, a whisper in the wind that made the hairs on the back of Aeryn's neck stand on end. A shadow moved in the distance, gliding between the trees with unnatural grace.

Thorne's eyes flashed to hers. "We're not alone."

Before Aeryn could react, the first arrow flew. It was a streak of flame, lighting up the night like a burning comet. She barely had time to raise her hand, deflecting it with a burst of fire that collided with the projectile, causing it to explode into embers midair.

But it wasn't just one arrow. Another followed, then a third. Each one more precise, more dangerous than the last. Aeryn's heart raced, and she could feel the fire inside her pulse in response, as though it too could sense the danger closing in.

"We're being hunted," Aeryn hissed, the fire licking at her palms, growing hotter with every passing second. She could feel the burn, the power within her, the force of the flames that had always been a part of her, yet something was different now. **Stronger.**

Thorne's eyes locked onto hers, his face a mask of icy determination. "Get ready," he said, his voice steady. "They'll be on us soon."

Before Aeryn could even respond, the forest erupted in a flash of red. Figures cloaked in shadows emerged from the trees, their movements swift and fluid. The assassins were upon them, drawn like moths to a flame.

Aeryn didn't wait for them to get closer. With a wave of her hand, the fire exploded outward, a raging inferno that lit up the night sky. Flames roared from her fingertips, a surge of heat that consumed the air around them. But her fire wasn't enough to stop them. The assassins were quick, moving in perfect synchrony, their eyes alight with an eerie focus. They were fire-wielders too, and their power was almost as strong as hers.

Aeryn's stomach tightened as she realized what she was facing. **More fire. More danger.**

"Thorne!" she shouted, her voice carrying over the roar of the flames. "We need to get out of here!"

But Thorne wasn't moving. He was standing his ground, his gaze fixed on the approaching figures. Aeryn could feel the pulse of his power—ice, cold, unyielding—radiating from him like a storm. Her own flames flickered and swirled in response to his presence, a strange harmony that both terrified and intrigued her. They were opposites—fire and ice—but together, they were something else.

Something deadly.

Thorne's eyes met hers again, and for the first time, Aeryn saw the faintest flicker of uncertainty in his gaze. But it was gone in a heartbeat, replaced by cold resolve.

"Stay close," Thorne ordered, his voice low and dangerous. "And don't stop fighting."

The assassins closed in on them, their hands outstretched, flames dancing between their fingers. Aeryn felt the heat rise in her chest, but it wasn't enough. They were too close. Too many.

And then, something inside her snapped.

Without thinking, Aeryn surged forward, her body igniting in a wave of blistering heat. Her fire exploded outward, expanding in a circle of flame that lit up the entire forest. The assassins faltered, their movements slowing as the heat from Aeryn's flames clashed with theirs. But it wasn't enough to stop them.

The next moment, she felt it—Thorne's power, merging with hers.

It wasn't just the cold. It was an unnatural force, like a blizzard sweeping across the land, crashing against her fire like a tidal wave. The two elements collided, creating a violent surge of energy that ripped through the forest. Aeryn's heart raced as the world around them blurred into a frenzy of ice and flame.

For a heartbeat, nothing made sense. There was only the fire within her, the ice around her, the explosion of power that surged between them like an unstoppable storm. The world trembled beneath the force of their combined powers.

And then the explosion came.

It was deafening—a shockwave of energy that tore through the trees, throwing them both backward. Aeryn felt the ground beneath her feet give way, and she was hurled through the air, her body slamming into a nearby rock with a sickening thud.

The forest around her was silent. She could taste the smoke in the air, feel the heat radiating from her body. But something was wrong. The power within her was still thrumming, still alive, but there was a sharp, dizzying edge to it. The fire, the ice, they had melded together, and now it was as though they had burned through everything in their path—leaving only destruction in their wake.

"Aeryn!"

Thorne's voice cut through the haze of smoke, and Aeryn blinked, her vision clearing. He was standing a few feet away, his eyes wild with something she couldn't place. His face was dusted with soot, his clothing singed, but there was no mistaking the look in his eyes. He was shaken, but alive. And for a moment, Aeryn wondered if she had imagined the devastation that had just occurred. The world around them was still, the trees scarred, but they stood untouched.

Thorne's gaze flicked to her, and for a moment, she saw the same fear mirrored in his expression. It was fleeting, gone in the blink of an eye, replaced by that cold, unyielding mask he wore so well.

"I didn't expect that," he muttered, the words thick with an unspoken understanding.

Aeryn struggled to her feet, the lingering tremor of her powers still pulsing in the air. "Neither did I," she replied, her voice hoarse. She could feel the heat inside her, but it wasn't the same. It wasn't just fire—it was something else, something more dangerous.

"You don't understand," Thorne continued, his voice now more urgent, his eyes scanning the destruction they had wrought. "If we keep this up, we'll burn everything. We'll freeze everything. Together, we're… we're too powerful."

Aeryn took a shaky breath, her heart racing. She could feel the weight of it in the air, the residual energy crackling between them like an invisible storm. The bond between them was undeniable now. The fire, the ice—they were two sides of the same coin. And when they combined, it was more than either of them could control.

"You're right," Aeryn said, her voice shaking as she looked at the scorched earth beneath her feet, the flames still licking at the trees. "We can't do this again. Not like that."

Thorne's eyes met hers, and for the first time, she saw something there—a vulnerability, an understanding that neither of them had chosen this. They hadn't chosen to be bound together by this impossible force. But now, there was no escaping it.

"We need to keep moving," Thorne said after a long pause, his voice firm once more. "We can't stay here. The explosion will have drawn attention."

Aeryn nodded, swallowing hard. The fire inside her was still smoldering, barely contained. But she knew he was right. The danger wasn't over. They were still in enemy territory, and their enemies had seen what they were capable of.

"Let's go," she said, her voice steadying as she moved toward him. Together, they walked into the night, the flames and ice still swirling in the air around them, a constant reminder of the power they had unleashed—and the danger that came with it.

But Aeryn knew one thing for certain now: no matter what came next, they couldn't stop. The bond between them had been forged in fire and ice, and together, they were unstoppable. But they were also a ticking time bomb, and they had no idea what would happen when it finally exploded.

The first flame had been ignited. The future was uncertain. But one thing was clear—together, they would either save the world or destroy it.

The air around them crackled with an energy that refused to die, the remnants of their combined powers hanging like a storm in the distance. Aeryn could feel it beneath her skin, like a pulse, a hum of heat and ice that flowed together in an unsettling harmony. The fire that had once been her most trusted ally now felt dangerous, like a beast waiting to be unleashed. And Thorne—his presence beside her felt equally tumultuous. They were walking through a storm, their bond both a shield and a threat.

Aeryn's heart still raced, her mind trying to process what had just happened. The explosion had been beyond anything she had ever experienced. She had used her fire before, with great force and precision, but the surge of energy when combined with Thorne's icy magic had been… overwhelming. It wasn't just the power. It was the aftermath, the way her body felt like it was vibrating with the strength of it, as though the universe had bent to their will.

"What was that?" she asked, her voice strained, as though she wasn't entirely sure if she was speaking to herself or to Thorne. "That… explosion. I've never—"

"Neither have I," Thorne interrupted, his voice low and tense.

His steps were slower now, his body more alert. They were both on edge, their nerves still crackling from the battle they had just fought. "I've never seen anything like that."

Aeryn turned her gaze to him. His usually impassive expression was cracked, revealing something deeper, something more vulnerable beneath the mask. His eyes, normally cold and detached, now held a flicker of something darker. There was fear there—something Aeryn hadn't expected.

"Do you think it's dangerous?" she asked, her voice quiet but edged with the weight of the question.

Thorne didn't answer immediately. He kept his gaze forward, his eyes scanning the darkened landscape, watching for movement. It was as if the world around them had turned into a waiting predator, its eyes trained on them, ready to strike at the slightest sign of weakness.

"I think we've crossed a line," Thorne said finally, his voice thick with hesitation. "We don't know what we're capable of. Together, we're not just fire and ice. We're something else entirely. Something… more."

Aeryn's stomach twisted at his words. Something **more**—that was exactly the problem. She had always known that her powers could be dangerous. Her fire, when left unchecked, could destroy entire villages. But this—this raw, uncontainable force that had been unleashed between them was something else. It felt like a bond forged in chaos, in destruction, and no matter how much she tried to fight against it, she could feel the pull between them.

She swallowed hard, forcing herself to focus on the path ahead. "We can't let this happen again," she said, her voice sharp with determination. "We have to figure out how to control it. To control **ourselves**."

Thorne nodded, but there was no certainty in his expression. His lips pressed into a thin line, his jaw tight with the weight of unspoken words. It was clear that he was just as troubled by their shared power as she was, if not more so.

"I don't know how," he admitted, his voice barely above a whisper. "But I will try."

Aeryn glanced at him, catching the quiet vulnerability in his words. There was more beneath his stoic exterior than he let on. She had always thought of Thorne as

Five

Betrayal Within

The night had fallen with an eerie stillness, the kind of silence that suffocated every breath, every heartbeat. Aeryn and Thorne had traveled far from the safety of the forest's edge, their feet crunching through the frost-covered ground as they made their way toward a secluded camp. The air was bitter, colder than it had been since they crossed the borders into the enemy's territory. The biting winds whipped through the trees, howling like a distant, angry cry, carrying with it an unsettling weight.

Aeryn felt it in her bones—the growing sense of unease that had been creeping over her since their encounter with the fire-wielding assassins. She couldn't shake the feeling that they were being watched, hunted by something far more dangerous than the assassins they had just defeated. The world around them felt too quiet, too still, as though everything was waiting for something to happen. Something catastrophic.

Thorne walked ahead of her, his long strides echoing through the night. He was a shadow in the darkness, his features cast in the harsh light of the half-moon. His silhouette was familiar, but tonight, Aeryn felt something strange—something she couldn't put into words. The way he held himself, the tightness in his jaw, the look in his eyes—it was all different, as if something had shifted within him.

"Thorne," she called softly, her voice cutting through the silence. "We need to talk."

He didn't stop, but his shoulders stiffened. "Not now, Aeryn," he replied, his voice distant, colder than usual.

Aeryn's stomach twisted with a mix of frustration and concern. She had known Thorne long enough to understand when something was wrong, when the mask he wore slipped, even if only for a moment. And tonight, there was no mistaking it—he was hiding something.

She quickened her pace, catching up to him with ease, her boots crunching on the snow beneath her. "What's going on?" she asked, her voice low, almost a whisper. "Something's changed. You've been distant for hours."

Thorne didn't meet her gaze, his eyes scanning the surrounding forest as though looking for something—or someone. "We've been through a lot. We both have," he said, his tone flat. "I'm just thinking about our next move."

Aeryn stepped in front of him, blocking his path. She wasn't going to let him shut her out again, not this time. She had been a part of this journey since the beginning, and she had a right to know what was happening.

"No," she said firmly. "You're hiding something, and I deserve to know what it is. What's wrong, Thorne?"

For a moment, he didn't say anything. His gaze flickered to

her, his icy blue eyes dark and unreadable. She could feel the weight of the silence between them, the tension thick enough to suffocate. The crackling fire from their campfire seemed distant, almost irrelevant in the face of the storm brewing between them.

"Aeryn," Thorne finally spoke, his voice low and almost regretful. "There's something I haven't told you. Something about me. About my past."

Aeryn's heart skipped a beat. The way he spoke, the look in his eyes—it was a confession, a revelation that she wasn't prepared for.

"What do you mean?" she asked, her voice barely above a whisper. The chill of the night seemed to press against her, her breath coming in shallow bursts as the weight of his words sank in.

Thorne hesitated, his gaze flickering to the dark expanse of trees ahead. "I don't want to involve you in this. It's not your fight."

But Aeryn wasn't going to back down. Not now, not when it was clear that something crucial was being hidden from her.

"Thorne, whatever it is, I'm already involved. We're in this together."

His eyes met hers, and for a moment, there was a flicker of something—something vulnerable, something almost… human. It lasted only a moment before he hardened again, the mask slipping back into place.

"It's my family," he said quietly, his voice strained. "The truth about them. About what they did."

Aeryn's mind raced, her heart pounding in her chest. Thorne's family was powerful—ruthless even—but she had never imagined the depth of the darkness that surrounded them. She had always known there was more to Thorne's icy exterior than he let on, but this…

"Your family?" she repeated, trying to process what he was saying. "What did they do?"

Thorne took a deep breath, his gaze dropping to the snow at his feet. "It's not something I've ever told anyone. But my father… he was part of the conspiracy that tore this world apart. The war between Fireborn and Iceborn, the bloodshed, the betrayal—it was all part of his plan. He's the reason this prophecy even exists."

Aeryn felt her stomach drop. She knew that Thorne's father had been a figure of immense power, a man whose reputation was both feared and respected. But to hear Thorne speak of him with such disdain, such hatred—it was like a blow to her chest.

"And you?" she asked, her voice barely above a whisper. "What about you? What part did you play in all of this?"

Thorne's jaw tightened, the muscles in his neck visibly flexing as he struggled with the words. "I was too young to understand. Too naive to see what was really happening. But I… I was part of the plan. My blood—my power—it was meant to be the catalyst that would destroy the other side, to finish what my father started."

Aeryn's breath caught in her throat. The realization hit her like a thunderclap. "You… you were the weapon."

Thorne's eyes flashed with a mixture of regret and anger, but he didn't deny it. "Yes. I was meant to be the one to tip the scales, to be the last piece of the puzzle."

Aeryn took a step back, her mind reeling. She had known that Thorne's past was complicated, but this… this was more than she had ever imagined. The fire that burned in her veins flickered, confused, as if it couldn't comprehend the betrayal that now lay between them.

"Why didn't you tell me?" she asked, her voice trembling. "Why didn't you warn me about this?"

Thorne's gaze softened, but his expression was still hard, his eyes distant. "Because I didn't want you to see me the way I see myself. I'm not the man I was before, Aeryn. I'm trying to break free of it. But the past—my father—he still has his hands on me, even now."

Aeryn stood there, frozen, her mind spinning with the weight of his words. They had been walking this path together, side by side, facing dangers she could never have imagined. But now, with this new truth hanging between them, the ground beneath her feet seemed to shift. How much of what they had shared was real? How much of it had been built on lies and secrets?

Before she could speak, a rustling sound broke through the stillness. Both Aeryn and Thorne immediately tensed, their bodies going rigid. Their hands hovered near their weapons, ready for whatever was coming.

From the darkness of the trees, a figure emerged—a silhouette too familiar to be ignored. Aeryn's heart skipped as she recognized the person stepping out from the shadows.

Riven.

Aeryn's breath hitched. Riven, the one who had been traveling with them for days, the one who had seemed so trustworthy. He had always kept his distance, had always been a quiet presence. But now, seeing him approach them with that same unreadable look in his eyes, she couldn't shake the growing sense of dread that settled over her.

"I thought I heard you two talking," Riven said, his voice cool, detached, as if nothing had changed. "But I didn't realize it was a confession."

Aeryn's pulse quickened. The last time she'd seen Riven, he had been standing at the edge of the camp, his eyes watching her from the shadows. He had always been a mystery, but something was different now. His casual tone, his lack of surprise—it didn't sit right with her.

"Riven," Thorne said, his voice colder than usual. "What are you doing here?"

Riven's lips curled into a smile, but there was no warmth in it. "I'm just making sure you two are still on the same side. After all, a little paranoia never hurt anyone, right?"

Aeryn's heart skipped. She could feel it now—the shift in the air, the weight of suspicion settling over them like a cloak. Something was wrong. Deeply wrong.

Thorne's posture stiffened beside her, his eyes narrowing. "What do you mean by that?"

"Oh, come now, Thorne," Riven continued, stepping closer. "You didn't really think I'd just follow you without questioning your motives. I've seen what you can do, what she can do. And I've heard whispers about what's coming. The prophecy. The plan. You're both players in a game much bigger than you realize."

Aeryn's heart slammed in her chest. **Betrayal.** It was in the air, thick and palpable. She had trusted Riven. They had all trusted him.

But now, as he stood before them, the truth was dawning on her. **Someone in their midst was working with the enemy.**

Her fire burned hotter, brighter, as the fear coursed through her veins. The suspicion she had ignored, the coldness in Riven's eyes—it was all clear now.

Thorne's voice was low, dangerous. "What are you saying, Riven?"

Riven smiled, but it didn't reach his eyes. "I'm saying that the enemy has been closer than you think." His gaze flicked to Aeryn, and for the first time, she saw the malice beneath his calm demeanor. "I'm saying that you were never meant to succeed. And I'm saying that I've been sent to ensure you fail."

The world around them tilted. Aeryn's fire flickered in response, as if it could sense the danger closing in. The betrayal was no longer a whisper in the shadows—it was real, undeniable, and it was standing right before them.

The air around them seemed to freeze, the wind suddenly stilled as though the world itself had paused, holding its breath. Aeryn's mind raced as she processed Riven's words, her heart hammering in her chest. Betrayal. It cut through her like a blade. She had trusted him, had relied on him in their journey through treacherous lands. And now, standing before them, he was the enemy.

Thorne's posture shifted, his shoulders locking into place as his icy gaze narrowed. Aeryn could feel the cold radiating from him, the air around them chilling as if his very presence could freeze the blood in their veins. He stepped forward, his voice low and dangerous.

"You've been working with the enemy all this time?" Thorne's words were measured, the calm before the storm, but there was a vicious edge to his tone. His ice-blue eyes were colder than ever, his aura a wall of impenetrable frost.

Riven didn't flinch. He stood there, smiling—smiling as if this was all a game, as if this betrayal meant nothing. His eyes gleamed with a cold certainty, a twisted satisfaction in the power he had over them now.

"I wouldn't say working with," Riven said, his voice smooth, his grin stretching wider. "But I've been keeping an eye on things. You know, just making sure the plan goes according to schedule."

The words hit Aeryn like a blow to the chest. The plan. She couldn't understand it—why had he stayed with them, pretending to be their ally, all the while playing both sides? The betrayal was so profound it felt like a physical weight pressing down on her chest. But she wasn't about to back down. Her fire surged within her, the heat beginning to coil at her fingertips. She wouldn't let him make a mockery of them.

"Who sent you?" Aeryn's voice was sharp, cutting through the tension that thickened the air. "Tell us who you're working for, Riven."

Riven's eyes gleamed as he tilted his head, as if amused by her demand. "Ah, always the demanding one, Aeryn. But I think you already know the answer." His eyes flicked to Thorne. "The very blood that courses through your veins is a weapon— don't you get it, Thorne? You're not meant to be free. Your family's plan was always to use you, to ignite the flames of destruction."

Thorne flinched, but only for a moment. His icy gaze turned into something darker, more menacing. Aeryn could see it— the flicker of something buried deep inside him, the pain he hadn't fully processed. His family's betrayal had scarred him in ways she hadn't imagined. But now, Riven's words had pushed him to the edge.

"I am not my father," Thorne's voice was a low growl, barely restrained. His icy powers crackled beneath the surface, like a storm waiting to be unleashed. "You don't get to use my past against me. I will not be part of your plan."

Riven chuckled, an empty sound that echoed through the darkened forest. "Oh, Thorne, you don't understand. You're already part of the plan. You always have been."

Aeryn stepped closer to Thorne, her fire blazing in her chest, the heat rising in response to the danger that was so close. "If you think you can manipulate us, you're mistaken, Riven. Whatever your game is, it's over now."

Riven's eyes narrowed, and the smug smile faded slightly. "Oh, I don't think you fully understand just how deeply I'm embedded in all of this. The flames that burn in your veins, Aeryn, they were always meant to fuel the destruction. And Thorne? He's nothing more than a pawn. A very powerful pawn, but a pawn nonetheless."

Aeryn's mind raced. **This was bigger than they thought.** Riven wasn't just a traitor—he was part of something far darker, something that connected her to Thorne in ways she hadn't anticipated.

"You don't know anything about us," Aeryn snapped, her anger rising like a torrent. "You think you can control us? Think again."

Before Riven could respond, Thorne surged forward. The cold in his eyes was unmistakable—an icy fury that matched the storm brewing inside him. But just as he was about to reach Riven, something changed. A sudden shift in the air, a flicker of movement, and Aeryn's instincts kicked in.

"Thorne, wait!" she shouted, grabbing his arm before he could make a move. Her voice was urgent, filled with a strange unease that she couldn't explain.

Thorne stopped, his body rigid with tension. He looked at her, confusion flashing in his eyes for just a moment before he nodded, his breath coming in shallow bursts. It took everything in Aeryn to hold him back, to stop him from unleashing his fury on Riven. But something was wrong. The situation was shifting in ways that didn't make sense.

A soft sound reached her ears—a faint rustling in the trees, followed by the unmistakable clink of metal. And then, before she could react, a voice broke through the silence.

"Not so fast, traitor."

Aeryn spun, her fire flaring in her hands, only to stop short when she saw who had emerged from the shadows.

It was Niklas.

Aeryn's heart stopped for a beat. **Niklas?** What was he doing here? He was one of Thorne's oldest allies, a man they had both trusted. But now, as he stepped into the clearing, his eyes darkened with an expression Aeryn had never seen before. He was dressed in the same cold, calculating demeanor he always wore, but there was something different about him tonight. Something that set him apart.

"Niklas," Thorne said, his voice taut with suspicion. "What are you doing here?"

Niklas gave a small, humorless smile, his gaze flicking to Riven and then back to Thorne. "I came to see what was taking so long. I didn't realize I'd be walking into a family reunion."

Aeryn felt the hairs on the back of her neck rise. **A family reunion? What did he mean by that?**

Thorne's jaw clenched, the words he was about to speak caught in his throat. Aeryn could see it now—the flicker of realization in his eyes. Something wasn't right. Riven, Niklas, and now the weight of it all—the betrayal had just deepened.

"What is this?" Aeryn demanded, her voice shaking with frustration. "Why are you both here?"

Niklas stepped forward, his movements smooth and deliberate. "You're asking the wrong questions, Aeryn," he said, his voice low and laced with something dangerous. "The question you should be asking is why you're so quick to trust someone like him." He gestured toward Riven, his words dripping with venom.

"You're the one working with the enemy, Niklas!" Thorne's voice was a low growl, but there was something desperate in his tone now. "You've been playing us all along."

Niklas's smile faded, replaced by a cold, emotionless expression. "I've always been playing the game, Thorne. You were just too blind to see it. All of you have been blind. Every move I made, every step I took, it was all part of the plan."

Aeryn's heart dropped. **The plan.** The words echoed in her mind as she realized the truth—**they were surrounded.**

Niklas's eyes locked onto hers, and for a split second, Aeryn saw something in his gaze—a flicker of recognition, of regret. But it was gone as quickly as it appeared.

"You're both too caught up in the prophecy," Niklas continued, his tone sharp and final. "You think the prophecy is about fire and ice, about Thorne and Aeryn. But you're wrong. The prophecy is about much more than that. It's about control, power, and who gets to shape the future."

Aeryn felt her breath catch in her throat. What was he saying? She had always believed the prophecy was their fate—a battle they had no choice but to face. But now, with every word that Niklas spoke, she realized how little she truly understood.

"You're working for the ones who want to destroy us," Thorne said, his voice trembling with rage. "I should have known."

Niklas didn't flinch. "You were never meant to win, Thorne.

None of us were. You were always just a tool in a much bigger plan."

Riven stepped forward, his eyes gleaming with malicious intent. "And now the pieces are falling into place. You're not the heroes, Thorne. You're the villains in someone else's story. And you always have been."

Aeryn's pulse quickened. The weight of their words—their betrayal—was sinking in. She had trusted them both, believed that they were on the same side. But now, standing before her, they were enemies. And worse, **they had known all along.**

"What do you want from us?" Aeryn demanded, her fire roaring to life in her hands as she stepped forward, her eyes blazing with the heat of her fury. "What is it that you're after?"

Niklas's lips curled into a smile, but there was nothing friendly about it. "What we've always wanted, Aeryn. Control. Power. The future."

Thorne moved to stand beside her, his icy presence as unyielding as ever. He may have been shaken by the truth, but he was not going to let these traitors win.

"We will stop you," Thorne said, his voice a chilling promise. "We will stop all of you."

Riven and Niklas exchanged a look, an unspoken agreement passing between them, but neither of them seemed afraid. Instead, they looked almost… amused.

"The game is far from over, Thorne," Riven said, his eyes gleaming. "And you won't be able to stop it. Not when you're so deeply tied to the prophecy."

Aeryn's heart pounded in her chest. The battle for their lives had only just begun. And now, with betrayal from within their ranks, it felt like the very ground beneath them was slipping away.

Six

Into the Heart of Fire

The air in the Fireborn kingdom was thick with the scent of smoke and ash, the land stretching before them in a wild expanse of rugged terrain. The sky above was an endless canvas of crimson, streaked with fiery hues that cast an unsettling glow across the horizon. As Aeryn stepped forward, she could feel the heat rising from the ground, the fire beneath her feet pulsing like a living entity. Every step she took seemed to call the flame closer, the power in her veins thrumming in response to the land she had been born to—yet, somehow, the fire that had always been her ally felt far more dangerous now, as if it was testing her, pushing her, urging her to let go of her control.

Thorne walked beside her, his face set in a grim mask of determination, his eyes scanning the surrounding landscape with the vigilance of a warrior. The Iceborn prince was not at ease here, his unease palpable as the fire energy grew stronger, swirling around them like a storm. She could see the tension in his every step, the way his fingers twitched, as if desperate to call upon the cold, to freeze the raging heat that threatened to swallow him whole.

"Stay close," Aeryn said, her voice steady but her heart racing in the pit of her stomach. This was the moment she had dreaded, the moment when she would face the heart of her kingdom's power—the trials that would test her as no other had before. But this time, she wasn't alone. Thorne was with her.

Thorne's gaze flicked to her, his eyes darkened with a storm of conflicting emotions. His expression was unreadable, his usually composed demeanor now fractured with the strain of being so close to the heart of the Fireborn lands.

"You think I'm worried about the trials?" he said, his voice low, tinged with the coldness of his usual sarcasm. "I'm more concerned about you."

Aeryn's heart skipped. She turned her gaze to him, her lips parting to respond, but the words died in her throat. His eyes were filled with something she couldn't place—something deep, something raw. She had always known him as the unyielding Iceborn prince, but here, in the midst of the fire, something within him was shifting, something that made him seem more vulnerable than she had ever seen him.

"Don't worry about me," she finally said, her voice a little too shaky. "Worry about yourself."

Thorne's lips quirked, but the smile didn't reach his eyes. "Trust me, I have no intention of letting the fire consume me."

Aeryn could feel the fire in her chest flare, the warmth rushing through her, pushing against the cold she had always known, but there was no time to dwell on it. Ahead of them, the great gates of the Fireborn kingdom loomed, massive iron structures adorned with intricate designs of flame and phoenixes. It was said that these gates were not just a barrier, but a symbol of the Fireborn's strength—a reminder that the fire was both their power and their curse.

As they approached, the ground beneath their feet seemed to pulse, the very earth beneath them alive with heat. The gates creaked open slowly, the sound like a roar, and beyond them lay a desolate landscape—flame-scorched earth and crumbling ruins, the remnants of an ancient civilization that had once been as powerful as it was ruthless.

"The trials begin here," Aeryn said softly, her voice heavy with the weight of what was to come.

Thorne looked at her, his eyes full of questions. "What kind of trials?"

"Ancient rites," she said, her voice quiet but firm. "They test every Fireborn who wishes to ascend to their rightful place. It's not just about power—it's about survival."

Thorne's expression darkened, but he didn't say anything. Instead, he stepped closer, his presence an anchor beside her in the face of the unknown. Aeryn was grateful for it. She had always feared facing these trials alone, but now, she wasn't. Now, there was a bond between them—one forged in the heat of battle and tempered in the cold of betrayal.

Ahead of them, a figure appeared—an old woman, cloaked in flames that flickered and twisted like a living thing. Her eyes, though aged, burned with a fierce intensity, as if she had seen countless generations of Fireborn pass through this very trial. She regarded Aeryn and Thorne with a mixture of expectation and disdain.

"You've come," the woman said, her voice like the crackling

of fire. "But only one of you will walk away from this."

Aeryn's stomach twisted. She had heard the stories. The trials were not just a test of strength—they were a test of will. Many Fireborn had come before her, only to be consumed by the flames. The trial would show them who they truly were, who they were meant to be.

"You can still turn back," the woman continued, her gaze flicking to Thorne with a look that seemed to pierce him through. "The fire here will burn you. It will not differentiate between friend and foe."

Aeryn didn't move, didn't flinch. She had already made her choice. Her eyes locked with the woman's, and she took a step forward, her feet planted firmly on the scorched earth.

"I'm ready," she said.

The woman's lips curled into a smile, though there was no warmth in it. "Very well. But know this, Fireborn princess, your destiny is tied to more than just fire. It is bound to the one who stands beside you." Her gaze shifted toward Thorne, her eyes narrowing. "And that bond will either save you or destroy you."

The ground shook beneath their feet, and the fire surged in response, the flames twisting like serpents around them. Aeryn felt her power flare to life, the heat growing within her until it felt as though the very air was burning with her. But Thorne... he was struggling. She could see it—the way he clenched his fists, the way his body tensed as the heat pressed against him, as though the very fire was an enemy he couldn't escape.

"Thorne," Aeryn said, her voice barely above a whisper. "You need to control it. You need to fight back."

Thorne's face was pale, the veins at his temples visible as he struggled to breathe, his eyes filled with the growing panic of the heat that threatened to consume him. "I can't," he rasped, his voice low and strained. "I can't control it. Not like this."

Aeryn felt a surge of fear, a deep, primal terror. She couldn't lose him here—not now, not when they had just begun to understand what their bond truly meant. She stepped forward, her fire flaring out of her, a wave of heat that rippled across the ground and crashed into Thorne's body.

"Focus," she commanded, her voice strong despite the fear threatening to overtake her. "We're in this together. Let me help you."

Thorne looked at her, his eyes filled with something she hadn't expected—something that made her heart skip. There was a vulnerability there, a rawness that tore through the walls he had built around himself. And in that moment, she realized something—this wasn't just about power. It was about trust. The kind of trust that went beyond anything they had ever shared before.

He nodded, his voice barely a whisper. "Help me."

Aeryn reached out, her fire sparking around them, wrapping itself around Thorne's form like a protective shield. She felt his power, his cold, surge against hers, and for a moment, it was like they were two halves of the same whole—opposites, yes, but united in their struggle.

Her fire entwined with his ice, the two forces colliding and merging, and the earth beneath them trembled. The flames burned brighter, hotter, but Thorne's ice held steady, a cold foundation that anchored them both. Together, they were a force unlike anything either of them had experienced before. The world around them seemed to fade, and in that moment, they were everything and nothing.

The ground cracked beneath them, the very earth screaming in protest as the power surged. Aeryn could feel it—the push and pull of fire and ice, the way their energies collided and threatened to explode. But it wasn't just destruction. It was creation, too.

With a final, guttural cry, the earth beneath them split open, and a massive burst of flame shot toward the sky, the heat scorching everything in its path. The blast sent them both flying backward, their bodies colliding with the ground as the fire roared around them. Aeryn gasped for breath, her chest heaving as she tried to steady herself, her body trembling from the force of the explosion.

Thorne was beside her in an instant, his hand on her arm, steadying her. She looked at him, her eyes wide with disbelief, but there was something else there, too—a shared understanding. They had done it. They had harnessed their powers, united them in a way that neither of them could have predicted.

The woman who had guided them through the trial stood in the distance, her expression unreadable. The flames still flickered around her, but her eyes were locked on Aeryn and Thorne with a piercing intensity.

"You've passed the first trial," the woman said, her voice a strange mix of awe and fear. "But be warned, Fireborn… The trials ahead will not be so kind."

Aeryn struggled to her feet, her heart still racing, but a sense of relief washed over her. She had done it. They had done it. They had survived the first test.

But even as she stood, the weight of the prophecy loomed over them, heavy and unyielding. They were far from finished, and the trials were far from over. Whatever lay ahead, Aeryn knew one thing for certain: she and Thorne were bound together by more than just fate. They were bound by fire, by ice, and by something much more powerful than either of them had fully realized.

As they stood together, the flames of the Fireborn kingdom flickering at their backs, Aeryn's heart ached with the unspoken truth—no matter what came next, their bond would either save them or destroy them.

And they would have to face it together.

The air around them shimmered with residual heat, the flames from the trial still licking the sky, casting long shadows across the land. Aeryn's chest rose and fell with the effort of regaining her breath, but there was a strange sense of clarity within her. They had survived, yes, but the cost of it was still settling into her bones. The heat, the fire, the power that had surged between her and Thorne—it was all too much to comprehend in the span of a few moments.

She could feel the weight of his presence beside her, could sense the strange bond that had formed between them in that explosion of fire and ice. They had crossed a line. Aeryn wasn't sure if it was a line of survival or something deeper, something irrevocable. They had shared power, combined their forces in a way that had shaken the very foundations of the earth beneath them.

Aeryn turned to Thorne, her gaze catching his for a moment. His expression was unreadable, his icy mask slipping back into place as he stood tall beside her. He hadn't said a word since the trial had ended, and though his eyes were as cold as ever, there was something in the way he held himself now—something changed.

"Are you alright?" she asked softly, the question slipping from her lips before she could stop herself.

Thorne glanced at her, his eyes narrowing just slightly, but he didn't answer immediately. His lips twisted into a brief smile, though it lacked warmth. "I'll be fine," he said, his voice cool, though there was a flicker of something behind his words—a vulnerability that Aeryn wasn't used to seeing.

She stepped closer to him, drawn by the same strange pull that had been growing between them since they first met. Her fire still simmered beneath her skin, but now it was calmer, more contained. The danger of the trial had been replaced by something more profound. She could feel it in the air, a crackling tension that seemed to emanate from both of them.

Thorne stiffened slightly as she approached, but Aeryn didn't miss the subtle shift in his gaze, the way his breath hitched ever so slightly. She wasn't sure if he was aware of the way their bond had deepened in the wake of the trial, or if he was simply trying to suppress it, just as he had been suppressing the fire inside him.

"We should keep moving," Thorne said abruptly, his voice pulling Aeryn back to the present. "The trials aren't over."

She nodded, though a part of her wanted to linger, to say something—to acknowledge the unspoken understanding between them. But there was no time for that now. The woman who had guided them through the trial was still standing in the distance, her presence like an ominous shadow at the edge of their vision.

Aeryn's heart skipped as she turned toward the woman. The Fireborn matron's eyes glinted in the dimming light, an inscrutable expression on her face as she watched them, as though waiting for something—waiting for a sign of what came next.

"You passed the first trial," the woman said, her voice low and cutting through the stillness of the night like a blade. "But there are more, Fireborn princess. More that will test not just your power, but your very soul."

Aeryn swallowed hard, her throat dry. The prophecy still hung over her, over them both, like an unyielding storm cloud, ready to break. She could feel the weight of it pressing against her chest, suffocating her. The fear had been there since the first trial, since she first heard the ancient words—the prophecy that told them one would burn with fire, the other freeze with ice.

But the trial had done something to her, something that made her question everything she had believed. She wasn't alone in this. Thorne—Thorne was with her, his strength, his coldness, his icy power. They had been forced together in the face of this greater force, but the way their powers had merged—it had been something more than survival.

"I'm ready," Aeryn said, though her voice wavered. She didn't know if she was ready for the trials, or for what lay ahead. But one thing was certain—she couldn't turn back now.

The woman regarded her with an inscrutable look. "Ready or not, the heart of fire awaits you. And if you fail… if you falter… both of you will be consumed."

Aeryn's breath hitched. She glanced at Thorne, seeing the same flicker of doubt in his eyes, though he masked it quickly with the coldness that was so familiar to him. There was no turning back. The trials had already begun. They had stepped onto the path, and now they had to walk it together.

The woman stepped aside, gesturing for them to follow her deeper into the heart of the Fireborn kingdom. The ground beneath them seemed to pulse with every step, the heat of the land rising to meet them like a living thing, an overwhelming force that sought to burn them, to test them. It wasn't just a test of power—it was a test of who they were, of their very souls.

As they walked, the land around them grew more desolate, the ruins of ancient Fireborn structures rising from the ashes like forgotten monuments. Aeryn's mind raced with the history of this place—the rituals, the sacrifices, the legends of those who had tried and failed before her. She could feel the weight of it all pressing on her, threatening to overwhelm her. This was her kingdom, her birthright. But it was a birthright tainted by blood, by fire, by the very force that had been used to control her people.

They came to a vast, open expanse, the ground cracked and broken as though some great force had torn it apart. In the center of the expanse stood a towering stone pillar, its surface covered in intricate carvings that seemed to writhe in the dying light of the day. The flames that danced along the edges of the pillar pulsed, flickering like a heartbeat, but they did not spread. They remained contained, controlled.

The woman stopped at the base of the pillar, turning to face them. Her eyes gleamed with a sharp intensity as she regarded them both. "This is the Trial of Fire," she said, her voice low. "Here, you will face your greatest fears—your inner demons— and the flames that have consumed your people. This is the trial that will determine if you are worthy to survive."

Aeryn felt her heart clench at her chest. **Her greatest fears.** What did that even mean?

"You must both enter the flame," the woman continued, her gaze now flicking to Thorne. "But only one may emerge unscathed. Only one of you can pass the trial."

Aeryn turned to Thorne, her breath catching. She could feel the intensity in the air, the danger that radiated from the flame. She could feel the power of it calling to her, urging her to step forward, to face what lay ahead. But her heart thudded in her chest. **What did this mean for them?**

Thorne's icy eyes met hers, his jaw tight. "We've come this far," he said, his voice a low growl. "We won't fail now."

Aeryn nodded, but there was still doubt lingering in her chest. **What would the fire reveal about them? What would it force them to face?**

The flames before them seemed to grow taller, hotter, as if sensing their hesitation. The pulse of power within her flared once more, her fire screaming for release, but she couldn't just give in. Not now. Not when they were on the edge of something far greater than either of them understood.

With a deep breath, Aeryn stepped forward, her fire swirling around her, hot and bright, but controlled. Thorne followed, his own icy presence like a cold front moving in, but together, they moved toward the pillar.

As they reached the base of the pillar, the fire flickered and swirled around them, pulling them into the flames. Aeryn's heart raced, the heat of the flames searing her skin, the very air alive with power. She felt herself being pulled in, swallowed by the fire that seemed to wrap itself around her body, drawing her deeper and deeper into the heart of the flames.

For a moment, she was lost, surrounded by the roaring fire that blurred everything around her. Her heart pounded in her chest, her breaths shallow as the heat seemed to consume her, her body pushing against the fire, desperate to break free. But the flame wasn't just physical—it was something more, something deeper.

And then, from the darkness, she heard a voice.

"Aeryn."

She spun, her body tense with fear.

Thorne's voice echoed through the flames, but when she turned, he was nowhere to be seen. The fire twisted around her, like a thousand whispers, and she reached out, her fingers grazing the edges of the flame. **Where was he?**

"Aeryn."

Her name again, this time closer. She couldn't see him, couldn't find him, but the sound of his voice was unmistakable.

"Thorne!" she shouted, her voice swallowed by the flames.

But no answer came. Only the roaring fire, the consuming heat.

And then, with a surge of power, Aeryn's fire exploded from within her, a fierce, uncontrollable wave that pushed the flames back, creating a path forward. Her pulse quickened as she felt the weight of her powers shifting, changing. She had to find Thorne. Had to make it through the fire.

But what would it cost them?

In that moment, she realized one undeniable truth—this was only the beginning. The flames had been testing her, testing them both. And the true trial was yet to come.

Thorne's presence—his power—was the only thing that could guide her through. Together, they could survive the fire.

But they would have to confront their deepest fears to do so.

Seven

The Tides of Trust

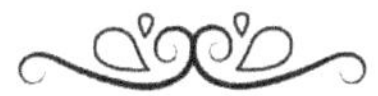

The flickering light of their campfire cast long shadows across the barren landscape. The heat from the flames had a false comfort to it—an illusion that everything was fine when, in truth, it was anything but. Aeryn could feel the weight of it, heavy in her chest. The fire, once a familiar comfort, now felt like a threat. Every flicker of heat reminded her of the choices she had yet to make, the ones that would decide everything.

She stared into the fire, her fingers tingling with the raw power that simmered beneath her skin, ever-present, ever-dangerous. It had been days since they had crossed into the heart of the Fireborn kingdom, but the trials she had faced there had left their marks on her—marks that only she could see. She had survived, yes, but at what cost?

The night had fallen into an unnatural stillness, the kind of quiet that precedes a storm. The wind was absent, and the ground beneath them was frozen solid, as though even the earth held its breath. Aeryn's thoughts churned, her mind unable to rest. The Fireborn king, her father, had made his intentions clear. His plan was to use her—**use her**—as a weapon to wage war on the Iceborn. He saw her fire as a tool, an unstoppable force that could tear through their enemies. And now, he intended to wield it for his own gain.

The thought twisted in Aeryn's stomach like a knife. She had always known that her powers came with a cost, that they would one day be used against someone. But to use them against the Iceborn? Against Thorne's people? It was an unforgivable betrayal of everything she had fought for, everything she had believed in.

And yet, she had been faced with a choice.

A choice that was already unraveling everything.

"Aeryn," Thorne's voice broke through the silence, low and guarded. She hadn't realized he was standing there, his silhouette outlined by the firelight. The tension in his voice made her shiver. "We need to talk."

Her heart skipped a beat, and she felt the familiar knot of anxiety tighten in her chest. She knew what this was about— had known it was coming. The betrayal, the secret she had been keeping, was about to be uncovered.

She turned slowly, her gaze meeting his. His face was a mask of cold determination, his eyes hard and unreadable. The fire between them had always been powerful, but now it felt like it might consume them both.

"I don't want to hide it anymore," Aeryn said, her voice barely above a whisper. "But I don't know what to do, Thorne. I don't know if I can stop it."

Thorne's eyes narrowed slightly, his jaw tightening as he

took a step closer to her. The air between them was thick with unsaid words, with tension that had been building since they first arrived in the Fireborn kingdom. She could see it in his eyes, the flicker of disbelief. He had trusted her, and now she had to explain why she had been keeping secrets.

"What are you talking about?" His voice was quiet but sharp, each word weighted with growing suspicion.

"The Fireborn king," Aeryn said, her voice cracking slightly. "My father… he wants to use my powers to attack the Iceborn. To wage war."

Thorne froze, his face going pale. For a long moment, neither of them spoke. The fire crackled between them, the only sound in the stillness of the night. Aeryn's heart hammered in her chest, each beat a painful reminder of the decision she had made.

"How could you—" Thorne began, his voice thick with disbelief. "Aeryn, how could you let him do this? How could you even think about it?"

Her stomach twisted at his words, his tone cutting deeper than she expected. He was angry—no, more than that. He was devastated. And she had no one but herself to blame for it. The man she had grown to care for, the man who had stood beside her through every trial, was now staring at her with a mixture of betrayal and confusion.

"I didn't have a choice, Thorne," Aeryn whispered, her voice trembling. "My father threatened everything I've worked for. He promised me power beyond anything I ever imagined if I did this. He told me he would destroy the Iceborn if I refused."

Aeryn felt her breath catch in her throat as the weight of the words hit her again. It wasn't just a choice of loyalty; it was a choice of survival. Her people were on the brink of collapse, and if she didn't comply, the war would be on her. She would be forced to watch as everything she had known crumbled before her.

"Then fight him," Thorne's voice cut through her thoughts, his anger rising. "Fight him, Aeryn. You don't have to do this. You don't have to give him what he wants."

She shook her head, the words lodged in her throat like stones. "You don't understand, Thorne. My father won't stop. He'll burn everything down to get what he wants. I can't fight him. Not alone."

Thorne stepped forward, his eyes dark with a mixture of pain and frustration. His fingers curled into fists at his sides, his body taut with the effort of holding back. "I've been fighting my entire life. I thought you understood that."

Aeryn felt the sting of his words like a slap across her face. She had always known the cost of power, but this—this was different. She was being torn between two worlds, and every step she took seemed to push her further from the one she had once known. Her heart ached for him, for the man she had come to trust, the man who had fought by her side through the flames.

"I understand more than you think," Aeryn said, her voice thick with emotion. "I understand that my loyalty to my people will always be questioned. But I can't be the one who destroys everything. Not again."

For a moment, Thorne said nothing, his eyes searching hers as if looking for some sign that she wasn't lost to him. The silence stretched between them, thick with tension, until he finally spoke, his voice tight and full of restraint.

"You've already made your choice, haven't you?" Thorne asked, his voice a whisper of disbelief.

Aeryn swallowed hard. "I had to. There was no other way."

Thorne's face hardened, his expression closing off. He took a step back, the space between them growing wider, colder. "So, you're willing to betray everything we've fought for," he said, his voice low and quiet, filled with an edge of hurt. "You're willing to sacrifice us—for what? Power? Safety?"

Aeryn's heart broke at the words. She knew she had made a terrible choice. She had never wanted this. But her world had been upended, her loyalty stretched too thin. The love she had begun to feel for Thorne, the bond they had formed through fire and ice, seemed to fade before her eyes.

"I never wanted this, Thorne," she said, her voice breaking. "But I'm trapped. I can't get out."

Thorne's face was like stone, his eyes filled with cold fury. He stepped back another pace, shaking his head, as if the pain of her betrayal was too much to bear. "I thought I knew you, Aeryn," he said, his voice barely above a whisper. "I thought you were different. But now… now I see that you're no better than your father."

The words cut through her, slicing through her chest like a blade. She staggered back, as if the weight of his condemnation had physically struck her. She had never imagined that his anger, his disappointment, would feel like this—like a chasm opening between them, an irreparable rift.

"I've made my choice," Aeryn whispered, her voice shaking, tears threatening to spill from her eyes. "I don't expect you to understand. I don't even understand it myself. But I thought… I thought you would stand by me."

Thorne looked at her for a long moment, his eyes filled with unspeakable pain. The silence between them was suffocating, an abyss too vast to cross.

"I don't know if I can," he said, his voice rough, broken. "How can I stand by you when you've turned against me? When you've chosen them over us?"

His words struck Aeryn like a physical blow, and she felt the ground beneath her feet shift. The world around her seemed to blur, the flames from the fire flickering in the distance, casting shadows that danced in her mind. She wanted to reach out, to explain, to tell him how much she regretted this, how she had been forced into a corner. But the words wouldn't come.

Thorne turned away, his back to her, the distance between them now a chasm that neither of them seemed able to cross.

"Aeryn," he said, his voice thick with regret. "You're right. I don't understand. And I don't think I ever will."

He walked away, his steps heavy, each one echoing in the silence between them. Aeryn stood there, frozen, as the weight of his words crushed her.

Her chest tightened, and for the first time, she realized that the future she had imagined—her place in the world, her love for Thorne, her loyalty to her people—was slipping through her fingers, just like sand in the wind.

She had lost him.

And she had lost herself in the process.

Aeryn stood motionless in the center of the clearing, the air around her thick with the weight of what had just transpired. Thorne's retreating figure was already a shadow in the distance, swallowed by the night, and the realization that he was gone hit her like a crushing blow. Her breath caught in her throat as she struggled to steady herself, her heart pounding in her chest, yet there was a hollow feeling spreading through her— the emptiness that came with the consequences of her actions.

She could feel the heat of the fire at her back, but it did nothing to warm her. The flames that had once been her ally now seemed distant, their warmth taunting her as she stood alone in the dark. **Alone.**

The word echoed in her mind, and with it came a rush of bitter regret.

She had made a choice. A choice that she thought would protect them all. But now, standing in the aftermath, she couldn't escape the gnawing doubt that she had just torn everything apart—everything she had fought for, everything she had believed in.

"Thorne," she whispered into the stillness, her voice barely carrying through the air. She didn't even know why she spoke his name. He was already gone, and there was no turning back.

But the silence that answered her felt like a suffocating weight, an abyss that seemed to stretch endlessly between them.

She needed to fix this. She had to.

Aeryn's eyes fluttered shut as she tried to gather her thoughts. She couldn't breathe for the crushing sense of loss pressing down on her chest. The fire, the one that had once ignited her passion and her drive, now felt foreign, dangerous—uncontrolled. She had allowed herself to be swept up in the currents of loyalty, of fear, of what-ifs, but now… now, nothing seemed clear.

There had to be a way to make this right. There had to be a way to undo what she had done.

With shaking hands, she wiped away the tears she hadn't realized were streaming down her face. She had been strong for so long, carrying the weight of her powers, her choices, and now it seemed the fire inside her would burn her alive.

Thorne's betrayal was no less than her own. She had torn through the trust between them, and now, it felt like there was no way to repair it.

But what if there was?

"What am I doing?" she murmured, her voice trembling. The realization hit her with the force of a tidal wave. She had been so focused on survival, on trying to protect everyone around her, that she had lost sight of what really mattered— her connection to Thorne. He was the one who had stood by her through every battle, every trial, and now, the one person she trusted was slipping through her fingers.

Her breath quickened, and she started walking. The urgency in her step was unmistakable. She wasn't going to let him walk away. She wouldn't let him go without a fight.

Aeryn reached the edge of the camp and stepped into the darkness, following the faint trail of Thorne's footsteps in the snow. The night was cold, the air sharp against her skin, but she barely felt it as she moved forward. Every step felt heavier, weighed down by the realization that she might lose him forever.

Her heart twisted in her chest. **He's the only one who understands me.**

The fire in her veins surged again, an echo of the power she had been forced to wield. It burned bright, a constant reminder of what she had left behind, what she had risked. And it only fueled her determination.

"Thorne!" she called, her voice carrying through the empty woods. But there was no answer. The wind whispered through the trees, as if mocking her, as if telling her that she was already too late.

And yet, she didn't stop. She couldn't.

The further she ventured, the more isolated she felt. The world around her seemed to press in, dark and cold, the weight of her choices heavier with every step. She knew she couldn't undo what had been done, but there had to be a way to make it right. A way to earn his forgiveness. She couldn't live with the idea that she had lost him forever.

Ahead, she saw a flicker of movement—slight but unmistakable. Thorne.

He was standing by the edge of the cliffs that overlooked the valley, his silhouette a stark contrast against the moonlit sky. He was alone, facing away from her, staring out into the vast expanse as if lost in thought.

Aeryn's breath caught in her throat. She stepped closer, her heart racing in her chest as she drew nearer. He didn't hear her approach, his form still and unmoving, but there was something in the way he stood that made Aeryn's stomach twist with anxiety.

She hesitated for just a moment before speaking.

"Thorne," she said, her voice quiet, almost pleading. "Please."

He didn't turn around, didn't acknowledge her presence. The air between them was heavy with unspoken words, emotions they had both been trying to bury.

"I made a mistake," Aeryn continued, her voice raw, trembling. "I was so afraid, Thorne. Afraid of losing everything—losing my people, losing you… I didn't know what else to do."

Finally, he turned, his eyes meeting hers, and for the first time, Aeryn saw the full weight of the hurt in them. The icy mask he had carefully constructed had cracked, revealing the pain beneath. But there was something else there too—a flicker of hesitation, of confusion, like he didn't know whether to trust her again.

"You don't get it," Thorne said, his voice hoarse. "You don't get what it feels like to trust someone completely, only to have them tear everything apart. You think you're the only one who's afraid? You think you're the only one who's fighting to survive?"

Aeryn's chest tightened. "Thorne, I never wanted to hurt you. I didn't think this through. I was so focused on doing what I thought was right that I didn't see what it would do to us. To you."

Thorne stepped forward, his face tight with the strain of trying to contain the anger, the hurt, the confusion that had built up between them. His hand clenched into a fist at his side before he forced it to relax.

"You've made your choice," he said, his voice quieter now, but no less painful. "And so have I."

Aeryn took a step forward, her heart pounding in her chest. "Thorne, please, don't turn away from me. I—"

"You don't get it," he repeated, his voice thick with emotion. "I can't keep doing this, Aeryn. I can't keep being dragged into your world of fire and ash. I can't trust you when you keep making decisions that could destroy everything we've built. Everything we've fought for."

His words hit her like a slap, each one cutting deeper than the last. She had wanted to protect them all, to protect him, but in doing so, she had broken the very thing she had been trying to save. She could see it in his eyes now—the pain, the anger, the betrayal. And it was because of her.

"I'm sorry," she whispered, her voice barely audible. "I wish I could take it back. I wish I could fix it."

Thorne's gaze softened for a fraction of a moment, but it was fleeting. "It's too late for that."

Aeryn's heart shattered in her chest. She had lost him. She could feel it in the way his eyes no longer searched hers with the same warmth, the same trust. He was slipping away, and she was powerless to stop it.

The silence stretched between them, heavy and unyielding. Aeryn felt the fire in her chest grow dim, the heat of her own powers no longer a comfort, but a burden. What had she done?

Thorne turned away again, his shoulders stiff, his back to her. "You've made your choice, Aeryn. You have to live with it now."

Aeryn stood there, frozen, unable to move, unable to speak. Her thoughts swirled in a whirlwind of pain, of regret, of loss. She had fought so hard for him, for them, but now, she was standing at the edge of everything, watching as it crumbled.

"Thorne…" she whispered, but he was already walking away, his footsteps heavy against the frozen ground.

And Aeryn knew, deep in her soul, that this was the end. The fire that had once burned so brightly between them was now nothing more than a dying ember.

She had lost him. Forever.

Eight

Shattered Heart

The wind howled through the valley, a bitter, freezing gust that cut through Aeryn's cloak as she stumbled forward, her boots crunching against the frozen earth. The sky above was a canvas of dark, swirling clouds, the moon hidden behind the thick curtain of storm. The Fireborn kingdom had never felt more suffocating, more hostile, than it did now. Each breath she drew seemed to tighten her chest, the weight of the prophecy bearing down on her with unrelenting force.

One must burn with fire. One must freeze with ice.

The words echoed in her mind, louder now than ever before, taunting her as she moved deeper into the wilderness. She had no destination, no purpose—only the need to escape. To run. To push away the crushing reality of her situation.

Thorne. She could still feel his presence, his anger, the betrayal that hung between them like an immovable wall. They had fought—no, they had shattered each other's trust, and now there was nothing left but the cold distance between them. Every part of her ached with the loss. She had never wanted to hurt him. Never. And yet, she had. She had turned against him, against herself, all in the name of survival.

But the worst part—the part that gnawed at her soul—was that the prophecy had been right. It had always been right. She had believed she could change her fate, but now, it felt like she was drowning in it, unable to escape the tidal wave of destruction it promised.

She stumbled, her foot catching on a jagged rock hidden beneath the snow. She gasped, her body jerking forward, but she managed to catch herself against the icy ground.

"Get up, Aeryn," she muttered to herself, her voice a low, desperate whisper. She couldn't afford to fall now. Not when everything was slipping through her fingers.

The fire inside her surged, a burst of heat that burned beneath her skin, and Aeryn closed her eyes, focusing on it. The flames had always been a part of her. But now, they felt different—uncontrollable, volatile, and like a curse. She was a weapon, a tool to be used by the very people she had sworn to protect. The fire within her had been weaponized, and she couldn't control it.

The thought twisted in her chest, the pain of it rising like bile. Her father—her people—they would never see her as anything but a means to an end. She had been born to bring destruction, to annihilate the Iceborn. It was in her blood, in her destiny.

But Thorne… Thorne had seen her differently. He had seen the person she could be, the one she had always wanted to be. And now, she had torn that trust apart.

Aeryn wiped her eyes, brushing away the cold tears that had

formed in the corners of her eyes. She didn't have time to dwell on her emotions. Not when every step she took brought her further from him, from the love they had shared.

She looked around, disoriented. She had been walking for hours, lost in the haze of her thoughts, and now the night seemed to stretch endlessly in front of her. There was nothing but darkness and the weight of her choices.

But then, through the storm, she saw it. A flicker of light in the distance.

Her heart skipped. It was him.

Thorne.

Without thinking, she began to move toward the light, her legs moving of their own accord, her pulse quickening. The flickering fire was like a beacon, pulling her back, pulling her to him.

But as she drew closer, the light faded, the flames dimming until there was nothing left but the cold, empty air. She stopped, confusion bubbling inside her. The light had vanished, leaving only the darkness.

"Thorne?" she called out, her voice trembling, but the wind swallowed her words, taking them far from her.

There was no answer.

She turned around in a panic, her heart thundering in her chest. The wind howled louder now, and the night seemed to close in on her. The crackling of fire was still ringing in her ears, but when she tried to follow it, all she found was emptiness.

The darkness swallowed her whole, and she froze in place. The feeling was suffocating, like she had lost him forever.

Was it already too late?

Aeryn shook her head, fighting against the sudden surge

of panic. No. She couldn't give up. Not now. She couldn't lose him, not after everything they had been through. The love they shared—the love that had once felt so certain, so powerful—was now slipping through her fingers like smoke.

But what choice did she have? The prophecy had already chosen. It had chosen them both, and no matter how much she tried to deny it, the weight of their fate was something neither of them could escape.

Somewhere in the distance, Thorne stood in the dark, his back to her. His breathing was heavy, each exhale sharp and ragged as the weight of his anger and hurt tore through him. He could still feel her. Her fire. Her presence.

But he had to push it all away.

He couldn't let himself get lost in her again. Not after what she had done.

The betrayal cut deeper than he had imagined. Aeryn had chosen her people, had chosen the war, and in doing so, had left him in the cold. He had always known she had power, knew the fire inside her could burn everything to the ground. But this… this was different. This was a betrayal of everything they had shared.

Thorne's fists clenched at his sides, the icy rage building inside him like a storm. The cold was his to control, but even he couldn't suppress the anger that churned beneath the surface. His heart was torn, his thoughts a storm of conflicting emotions. **Could he forgive her?**

A part of him wanted to believe that she was still the woman he had trusted, the one who had walked beside him through everything. But that part of him was slowly being buried beneath the weight of her choices. She had turned against him, turned against the bond they had forged in fire and ice.

He had to let her go. He had to let **all of it** go.

But when he turned to walk away, the familiar sound of her voice cut through the darkness.

"Thorne!"

The pain in her voice stopped him in his tracks. His heart twisted, and for a moment, he stood frozen in place, listening to the soft sound of her footsteps in the distance. She was closer now, her voice laced with desperation.

"Aeryn…" he whispered to himself. His pulse quickened at the sound of her voice.

He turned around, his body moving before his mind could catch up. There she was, standing just beyond the tree line, her eyes searching for him, wide and full of sorrow. Her face was pale, her hair wild from the wind, but it was the look in her eyes—the rawness, the vulnerability—that struck him the hardest.

"Aeryn," he breathed, his voice hoarse, but he couldn't move toward her. The distance between them felt insurmountable.

She took a step forward, but the distance between them remained. "I'm sorry, Thorne," she said, her voice barely above a whisper. "I didn't know what else to do."

Thorne's chest tightened, the weight of her words suffocating him. His eyes scanned her face, searching for some sign that she hadn't completely betrayed him. But the more he looked, the more he saw the woman he had fought beside—the woman he had loved—and the more the pain of her betrayal cut deeper.

"Don't say that," he said, his voice sharp, his breath coming in ragged bursts. "You knew exactly what you were doing. You chose them, Aeryn. You chose the war."

"I didn't want this, Thorne," she said, her voice breaking. "I thought I could stop it, I thought I could save us, but I was wrong. I don't know what else to do. I don't know how to fix it."

Thorne closed his eyes, pain flooding his chest. His heart—his loyalty—had been tested more times than he could count, but this… this was different. This wasn't just a test of survival. This was the final blow. The one that would either tear them apart or bind them together.

He shook his head, the coldness of his emotions almost suffocating. "You can't fix this. You've already made your choice."

The silence stretched between them, heavy and suffocating, until it was broken by the sound of her trembling voice.

"Thorne… the prophecy. It says one of us must die," she whispered, her words hanging in the air like a death sentence.

Thorne's eyes snapped open, his heart thundering in his chest. The truth of her words struck him like a blow. The prophecy had always been there, lingering over them like a shadow, but now it felt like a curse, one that would tear them apart.

"No," he said hoarsely, his voice trembling with the weight of the realization. "No, Aeryn. We can't—"

Aeryn took a step forward, her eyes meeting his with a mixture of fear and resolve. "We have to. We have no choice."

Her words were like a final echo, a cruel reminder of the fate that awaited them both.

Aeryn stepped closer to him, the distance between them closing, but even as she reached out, Thorne couldn't bring himself to move. They were standing at the edge of it all—the edge of their love, their trust, and their fate.

They couldn't escape it.

And they couldn't kill each other. Not yet.

Not until the prophecy fulfilled its cruel end.

Aeryn stood in front of him, her heart racing, her breath shallow, every part of her aching with the weight of the truth. The cold air between them seemed to grow colder, heavier, as the last of the distance between them closed. She wanted to reach out, to close the space between them completely, but something held her back. **What if this was the end?** What if nothing could repair the damage that had been done?

Thorne's face was set, his jaw clenched, the sharp angles of his features illuminated by the faint light of the fire behind him. His eyes were locked onto hers, but they were filled with something she couldn't decipher—something too painful for her to name. He hadn't moved when she had stepped closer, hadn't made any effort to reach for her.

And Aeryn didn't know what to do anymore. She had always known the prophecy would come for them, that it would demand a terrible price, but to hear the truth spoken aloud— the truth that one of them had to die—was like hearing the final verdict on their love. Their bond. The connection she had fought so hard to protect.

She felt the sting of betrayal again, not just from him, but from herself. She had chosen the war. She had chosen the Fireborn over the man who had stood by her side when no one else would.

"Thorne," she whispered, her voice breaking, "I never wanted this. I never wanted to hurt you."

For a long moment, there was nothing but the sound of the wind howling through the trees. The air around them was charged with an almost electric tension, as if the very earth beneath their feet was trembling at the thought of what they were being forced to face.

"I know," Thorne replied, his voice colder than the winter air, sharper than any blade. "But the question is, Aeryn, do you truly understand what you've done? Do you know what this means?"

Her heart twisted painfully. The question hung in the air like a weight, suffocating her. The truth was clear now, but so was the choice. **One must die.** The prophecy was no longer something distant, something that could be avoided or ignored. It was here, in front of them, a living, breathing reality.

"I'm trying to," she said, her voice trembling. "I know I've made mistakes. I know I've failed you. But I—I don't know what else to do. I can't undo the past, Thorne. I can't change the decisions I've already made."

He didn't speak right away, his eyes flicking over her with something that felt like a mix of pity and rage. For a moment, it seemed like he might say something, something that would cut through the thick wall between them. But instead, he turned away, his back to her as he walked a few steps forward. He didn't face her, and that distance—that cold, deliberate move—felt like the final blow.

"I can't do this," Thorne muttered, his voice low, as if speaking to himself. "I can't keep pretending like everything is fine when I know what we are. What you are."

Aeryn's heart sank. His words cut deep, deeper than anything she had ever felt. He was right. The fire that had always been a part of her, that had once made her feel alive, was now a curse—something that would destroy them both.

"Thorne, please—" Her voice cracked, and she forced herself to swallow the knot of emotion rising in her throat. "I didn't want this to happen. I didn't want the prophecy to come for us. I thought we had time, that we could find a way to change it. But now… now it feels like there's no way out."

His back still turned, Thorne's shoulders were stiff, his entire frame locked with tension. Aeryn could see the anger coursing through him, feel it building like an inevitable storm. She had pushed him away, betrayed his trust, and now he was paying the price for it.

"I can't look at you the way I used to," Thorne said quietly, though his words were laced with an anger that made her flinch. "I can't pretend like everything is okay when I know you've chosen your people over me. Over us."

Aeryn closed her eyes, a fresh wave of tears rising behind her lids, but she couldn't let them fall—not now. Not when she had already lost everything.

"You're right," she whispered. "I have chosen them. And I've chosen the war. I thought it was the only way to protect what was left of my kingdom. But in doing so, I lost you. I lost us."

She could feel the tremor in her voice, the ache in her chest growing with every word. The love she had once believed would conquer everything—the love that had burned so brightly between them—felt distant now, as though it had been extinguished by the weight of the prophecy and the weight of her own decisions.

Thorne didn't turn around. His silence was deafening.

She took another step forward, but he flinched, as if even her approach was something he couldn't bear. The movement stopped her in her tracks, a dagger of pain lodged in her heart.

"I never wanted to hurt you," she said softly. "But I did. And I don't know if I can fix it. I don't know if you can ever forgive me."

Thorne's shoulders tensed. The muscles in his back visibly tightened, but it wasn't until he finally spoke that she understood how deep his pain ran.

"You think I can forgive you?" His voice was low, venomous with the bitterness of a man who had been betrayed, a man whose heart had been shattered into pieces. "You've chosen your kingdom, Aeryn. You've chosen the power they promised you over the life we could have had."

"I chose survival," she whispered, tears now streaming down her face. "I chose to protect my people. I thought I could keep everyone safe. I thought if I did this, it would all be okay."

"It's not okay," Thorne shot back, his voice cracking under the strain. "It will never be okay, not when you've sold us out for power."

Aeryn shook her head, the weight of her guilt heavier than anything she had ever felt before. "I didn't mean for it to be like this. I didn't want the war. I didn't want any of it."

Thorne's eyes narrowed, a dangerous glint appearing in their ice-blue depths. "But you made your choice, Aeryn. And now we both have to live with it."

The bitterness in his tone made her chest ache. She reached for him, her fingers trembling, but he took a step back, his expression hardening further.

"You can't change the past," he said coldly. "And neither can I."

The wind picked up around them, howling as if in response to the devastation between them. The silence that followed was deafening, suffocating.

Aeryn stood there, trembling, her heart breaking as the man she had come to love—the man who had been her anchor through every storm—walked further away from her, each step a painful reminder of what she had lost.

"Thorne," she cried, her voice rising in desperation. But he didn't stop. He didn't even look back.

The words—the silence—felt like an unforgivable wound in her chest. She was standing on the precipice of everything, and she didn't know how to stop the fall. The prophecy had claimed its toll, had ripped them apart in ways she never imagined. She had made a choice, and now it felt like the price of that choice was too steep.

And then, in the distance, she saw it. The shadow of the future. The reason why they could never be whole again.

The prophecy had never been a warning.

It had always been a sentence.

The sound of footsteps echoed behind her, but she didn't turn. The truth was too much to bear.

She had no way to fix this.

And now, she had no one to help her face what was coming next.

Thorne had already chosen his path. And she had already chosen hers.

And they were both walking toward the end.

The Frozen Heart

The moon hung high in the sky, casting its pale light across the valley, illuminating the jagged edges of the cliffs that rose like silent sentinels around the Fireborn kingdom. The night was cold—colder than any she had felt before. Aeryn stood on the edge of the precipice, looking out into the darkness, her breath escaping in misty clouds that vanished into the void. The world was silent, except for the distant whisper of the wind, carrying with it a hint of what was to come.

The fire inside her burned, but it was a flickering, uncertain flame. It no longer felt like the raging inferno she had once known. The heat of her power had dulled, as if her heart itself had grown colder with each passing day. And in that silence, the weight of what had happened between her and Thorne hung like a pall, suffocating everything around her.

The prophecy had always loomed in the distance, but now,

it was a living, breathing thing. It had bled into their lives, dividing them in ways Aeryn had never anticipated. The rift between them felt like an insurmountable wall. Thorne, once the man who had fought beside her, had become a shadow of himself, trapped by his own fears, by the icy power that had always been his, but now threatened to consume him.

Aeryn clenched her fists, feeling the heat surge in her palms. Her fire had always been a part of her, an extension of her soul, but now, it felt foreign, distant. Her thoughts kept drifting back to Thorne, to the broken look in his eyes, to the distance he had placed between them.

He had isolated himself from her, from everyone, afraid that the rage of his powers would tear apart everything they had. He was afraid of becoming the very thing the prophecy foretold.

Aeryn closed her eyes, but the image of Thorne standing at the edge of the frozen forest—his back turned, his face a mask of cold indifference—was burned into her mind. She had tried to reach him. She had tried to close the gap between them, to pull him back from the brink, but nothing had worked. The harder she tried, the further he pushed her away.

Her heart ached, the guilt gnawing at her insides. She had made so many mistakes. She had chosen to protect her people, to honor the legacy of the Fireborn, but in doing so, she had broken the one thing she cared about most: Thorne.

The cold wind swept across the valley, and she shivered, pulling her cloak tighter around her shoulders. She couldn't lose him. Not like this. She couldn't let the prophecy tear them apart, not when they were the only hope for peace between their people.

But how could she reach him? How could she make him see that they were still fighting for each other, even if everything around them was falling apart?

Suddenly, there was a sound—soft, almost imperceptible, but it was enough to make her freeze in place. A footstep, the crunch of snow beneath a heavy boot. Aeryn turned, her heart leaping in her chest, her breath catching in her throat.

And there he was.

Thorne.

Standing in the shadow of the trees, his eyes locked on her, but they were distant—cold, empty, like the ice that ran through his veins. He had been keeping his distance from her for days now, and every time she thought she had found a way to reach him, he retreated further into the darkness of his mind.

"Aeryn," he said, his voice low and hollow, like the sound of wind howling through a desolate wasteland.

She took a step toward him, her heart pounding. "Thorne," she breathed, her voice trembling. "I've been looking for you."

He didn't move. He stood there, his arms crossed, the cold radiating from him in waves. She could feel the chill of his power even from this distance, an aura of ice and fury that seemed to pull the warmth from the air around him.

"You shouldn't have come," Thorne said, his voice barely a whisper, but it held a weight to it—an undercurrent of warning that she could feel deep in her bones. "It's not safe."

Aeryn's chest tightened, the words sinking into her like stones. "I'm not afraid of you, Thorne," she said, her voice stronger than she felt. "I'm afraid of losing you. I'm afraid of this… this distance between us. You've been shutting me out for days. I don't know how much longer I can take it."

Thorne's eyes flickered to her, but the coldness in his gaze never wavered. "I don't want to hurt you, Aeryn," he said, his voice barely audible, but the pain in it was clear. "I don't want to hurt anyone. But I can feel it, Aeryn. The power… it's overwhelming. I can feel it pulling at me, threatening to destroy everything."

Aeryn stepped closer, but her heart was heavy with the truth of his words. The last time they had been together, the fire and ice had collided, creating a storm of uncontrollable energy. She had felt it too—the way his icy powers surged in response to her own. But it was more than just the powers. It was the emotional weight they carried, the fear of the prophecy becoming true, of one of them having to die.

Thorne's eyes hardened as he watched her approach. "You don't understand," he said, his voice rising with the strain. "I can't control it. I don't want to become the monster in this prophecy. I don't want to hurt you, Aeryn. You don't deserve that."

She felt the surge of his power now, a cold wind that cut through her like a blade, and she stumbled back, the icy air clawing at her skin, stealing the warmth from her body. But it wasn't just the cold—there was something deeper, something darker in the way he spoke, in the way the ice surrounded him. He was fighting something inside himself, and she knew it was more than just the fear of his powers. It was the fear of losing control. Of becoming what he had always feared.

"You're not a monster, Thorne," Aeryn said, her voice shaking but determined. "You're not. The prophecy—"

"The prophecy is a death sentence," Thorne interrupted, his voice raw. "It's been there from the start. And I've been trying to fight it, but I don't know how much longer I can hold on. The rage, the cold—it's taking over."

Aeryn's heart wrenched at the vulnerability in his voice, the fear that had always been masked by his cold exterior. She had always known Thorne was stronger than he let on, that his power was more than just ice—it was his heart, the pain and anger he carried with him.

But she also knew this: Thorne had always been about control. He had controlled everything in his life, his powers, his emotions, his distance from others. But now, that control was slipping. The prophecy had cracked him open, exposed him in ways she had never seen before.

Aeryn took another step forward, reaching out to him, but he flinched, pulling away just as quickly. She could see the storm in his eyes, the icy wall he had built around himself, and she knew he wasn't going to let her through without a fight.

"I can't do this, Aeryn," he said, his voice trembling with a mix of anger and fear. "I can't keep pretending that everything is okay when I'm this close to losing myself. When I can feel the power building, threatening to tear us apart."

She reached for him again, her hand brushing his sleeve, but this time, he didn't pull away. He stood frozen, his body tense, his breath coming in shallow gasps.

"You don't have to do this alone, Thorne," Aeryn said softly, her voice laced with desperation. "I'm here. I'm not going to leave you. I'll fight this with you."

Thorne closed his eyes, the weight of her words pressing against him. For a moment, there was silence. Then, slowly, he spoke, his voice thick with emotion.

"You don't know what this will cost you, Aeryn," he said, his voice breaking. "You don't know what you're asking. The prophecy doesn't just take one of us—it's going to take everything."

She shook her head, her eyes searching his for any trace of

the man she had fallen in love with. "We'll find a way through it," she said, her voice unwavering. "Together. I'm not afraid of the prophecy, Thorne. I'm afraid of losing you."

The storm inside Thorne seemed to falter for a moment. His body softened, and for a brief second, the walls he had built around himself began to crack.

But then, just as quickly, the coldness returned, stronger than before. He stepped back, his expression hardening once again, the icy mask sliding back into place.

"I don't know if I can trust myself anymore," he said, his voice cold and distant. "And I don't want to hurt you."

Aeryn stood still, her hand still outstretched, the words she had hoped to say lodged in her throat. The ice around him was suffocating, and she could feel it—feel the coldness that was consuming him, piece by piece. He was fighting something inside him, something that was beyond their control. The rage, the power, the prophecy—it was tearing him apart.

But she couldn't give up on him.

She wouldn't.

"Thorne," Aeryn whispered, her voice breaking. "Please."

For a long moment, nothing changed. Then, with a movement so sudden it startled her, Thorne turned, walking toward the edge of the cliff. He stopped, standing at the precipice, his back to her, looking out into the storm.

Aeryn's heart ached with the weight of what was happening. She could feel the loss of him, the coldness that was swallowing him whole.

She had never been more afraid.

And yet, in that moment, she realized something. The prophecy wasn't just a curse—it was a choice.

And as much as the fire in her heart burned, it couldn't warm the frozen heart of the man she loved.

Not yet.

Thorne's shoulders trembled, and Aeryn could see the battle waging inside him. The ice, the fire, the rage—everything was crashing down upon them.

And neither of them knew which way they would fall.

Aeryn watched Thorne stand at the edge of the cliff, the weight of the moment settling over them both like a heavy fog. The wind howled around him, tousling his hair, but he stood motionless, as though the world itself had ceased to exist. She felt every inch of the distance between them now—the space where trust had once been, where warmth had once resided, and where love had burned brighter than either of their powers combined. But now, that love was extinguished, drowned in the icy abyss of fear and betrayal.

Could she reach him?

Her heart hammered in her chest as she took a tentative step forward, her feet sinking slightly into the snow with every movement. Each step seemed like a battle against the world itself, but she couldn't stop now. She had to try.

"Thorne," she called again, her voice wavering in the still night air, but this time, her words felt like fragile glass, ready to shatter under the pressure of everything left unsaid.

He didn't move.

Aeryn's chest tightened. **I've lost him.**

But the thought was unbearable. The bond they had shared, the promises they had made—it was all slipping away.

She was standing at the precipice too, just as much as he was. The storm inside her, the fury of the flames she had always controlled, began to rise again, but it was different this time.

It wasn't just the fire that raged within her. It was the fear, the guilt, the knowledge that she had caused this.

"Thorne, please!" she cried out, her voice raw with emotion. "You don't have to fight this alone."

For the first time, he turned to face her. But it wasn't the look she had hoped for. His eyes were distant, filled with an unreadable coldness. The walls were back in place, thicker than ever, and the distance between them felt insurmountable.

"You're still asking me to fight, Aeryn?" His voice was low, the words edged with a bitterness that cracked her heart further. "Do you even know what that would mean? To keep fighting against something that's already inside me? The rage, the power, it's all building. I can feel it. It wants to take control, and I can't stop it."

Aeryn's heart sank, her breath catching in her throat. "I'm not asking you to fight it alone," she whispered, her voice trembling. "I'm here. I'm not leaving you. Not now. Not ever."

Thorne's face tightened, and he turned away from her, his gaze fixing on the horizon. The wind whipped around them, a furious gust that swept the snow from the ground in great, swirling plumes. The tension between them thickened, like the calm before a storm. Aeryn could feel the pull of his power—the cold that radiated from him in waves—and her own fire stirred beneath her skin, responding to him like it always had, but now, it was more dangerous. She was beginning to understand what the prophecy truly meant.

Thorne was slipping into something she couldn't reach. **And if she didn't act now, she might lose him forever.**

"Thorne," she whispered again, taking another step toward him, closer this time. Her heart raced with fear—fear of losing him, fear of the prophecy, fear of the future they could never control. "I can't lose you. I won't. Please, listen to me."

For a long moment, he didn't respond. Then, just as she was about to speak again, Thorne turned sharply, his eyes flashing with a mixture of pain and fury. "You think it's that easy, Aeryn?" he spat, his voice rising with the storm inside him. "You think you can just come here and fix everything with your words? With your fire? You can't. You don't understand what it feels like to be torn apart from the inside out. You don't know what it's like to feel your own power becoming your enemy."

His words hit her like a physical blow, and she staggered back, but she didn't look away. The rawness in his eyes was unbearable. He was speaking the truth, but the pain was too much for her to bear. She had always known that Thorne was more than just his icy powers, that his heart was a battleground in itself. But this… this was worse than anything she had imagined. The rage, the fear of becoming the very thing he hated—it was tearing him apart.

"I know," Aeryn said softly, her voice breaking. "I know more than you think, Thorne. I feel the same fear. But I'm here. I'll stand by you, no matter what."

He shook his head, his expression hardening. "You don't get it. You don't understand the depths of what I am. The fire inside you—it's only a small part of what's coming. The prophecy, the power—it's bigger than us. It's bigger than anything we can control."

Aeryn took another step toward him, feeling the pull of his emotions, the cold that radiated from him like a storm ready to break. "I can't lose you," she repeated, her voice stronger this time, though it trembled with desperation. "We have to face this together. Whatever the prophecy says, we don't have to be its victims. We can choose. I'm choosing you."

Thorne's eyes flickered with something—something that might have been hope, but it was gone too quickly to be sure. He took a step back, and the coldness around him seemed to intensify, like an invisible barrier that pushed her away. His body trembled with the effort of holding it in, but she could see the struggle—the battle he was fighting against himself.

"You don't understand," Thorne whispered, his voice hoarse. "The prophecy says one of us has to die. I can't live with myself if I hurt you. And I can't live with the thought that the fire inside you might consume us both."

Aeryn felt her heart twist at his words, the pain of it almost unbearable. She had always known there was danger in their bond, but hearing it so clearly, hearing the truth of his fears—it broke her. The fire inside her surged in response to the pain in his voice, but she fought to keep it contained. **She couldn't let it burn him. Not now.**

"I won't let you face this alone," Aeryn said, her voice firm with the resolve she hadn't felt in so long. "We'll figure it out. Together."

Thorne closed his eyes, the weight of her words pressing down on him like a heavy stone. "I don't know how to trust you anymore, Aeryn. I don't know how to trust myself."

The words shattered the silence between them, and the world seemed to close in around her. The promise they had shared, the hope they had clung to, now seemed like fragile glass, about to break. But Aeryn wasn't ready to give up on him—not when she could still feel the bond between them, not when her heart still beat for him.

Thorne turned again, walking toward the edge of the cliff, his back to her. The cold emanated from him, his body tense, but he didn't look back. He didn't reach out.

And Aeryn knew, deep in her soul, that he was slipping away.

Tears pricked at the corners of her eyes, but she wiped them away angrily, her fists clenching at her sides. She couldn't lose him. Not like this. She wouldn't let it happen.

Her heart raced as she closed the distance between them, her fire beginning to flare again, the heat rising in her chest, but she wasn't going to let it burn out of control. She wasn't going to make the same mistake again.

"I'm not leaving you, Thorne," Aeryn said, her voice clear, though it trembled with the force of her emotions. She stepped forward, slowly, her presence steadying the crackling fire in her chest. "I'm here. You can fight it, Thorne. We can fight this prophecy together."

Thorne's shoulders stiffened as she reached out to him, but this time, he didn't pull away. His body trembled, not with the cold, but with something else—something she couldn't quite name. The ice, the fire, the prophecy—they were all swirling around them, an unavoidable force that seemed to drag them both toward a fate they couldn't escape.

"You don't know what you're asking of me," Thorne whispered, his voice hoarse. "You don't know what will happen if we do this. If I lose control…"

"I'm asking you to trust me," she said softly, stepping closer, her fingers grazing his frozen skin. "I'm asking you to trust us. I believe in you, Thorne. And I believe in us. We're stronger than this. We can find a way."

He didn't speak, but his eyes flickered to hers, something shifting beneath the ice. The walls he had built around himself were starting to crack, and for the first time, she could see the man she had fallen in love with through the cold fog that had clouded his heart.

The wind howled around them, the storm raging above, but it felt like the world had slowed, like they were standing in the eye of the storm. And in that moment, Aeryn knew that no matter what the prophecy demanded, they would face it together.

One step at a time.

The world was falling apart, but they weren't alone.

Not anymore.

Ten

Fire and Ice

The sound of marching boots echoed through the cold corridors of the Fireborn palace, their rhythmic thuds growing louder as Aeryn and Thorne made their way toward the throne room. The air inside was thick with tension, a suffocating quiet that pressed against them from all sides. Every step Aeryn took felt like a drumbeat to her heart—each one heavier than the last. The walls of the palace seemed to close in around her, their cold stone a grim reminder of the place she had once called home.

She glanced at Thorne beside her, his face a mask of cold determination, his eyes shadowed with something darker—fear, anger, or perhaps both. She couldn't tell anymore. The distance between them had only grown since they had arrived at the palace. The more she tried to reach him, the more he pulled away, as if the icy barrier around his heart had become impenetrable. The prophecy had done this to them. The fear of what they might become—what their love might destroy—was a constant weight on both of their shoulders.

"I'm not doing this for him," Thorne's voice broke the silence, low and strained. His words were directed to her, but his gaze was fixed on the path ahead. "I'm doing this to keep you safe, Aeryn."

She looked up at him, the flicker of vulnerability in his voice making her heart ache. His ice-blue eyes met hers for a brief moment before he looked away again, his jaw clenched.

"I know," she whispered, the weight of their unspoken fears pressing down on her chest. "I know, Thorne. But we can't keep running from this. It's time to face it."

They reached the heavy doors of the throne room, and Aeryn felt a surge of anxiety ripple through her. She had always known this moment would come—the moment when she would be forced to confront her father, the Fireborn king, and the role he expected her to play in his war against the Iceborn. The thought of it made her stomach churn. She had betrayed him. She had betrayed everything she had been taught to believe in.

Thorne placed a hand on the door, pausing for a moment before pushing it open. Aeryn stepped through first, her heart pounding in her chest. The throne room was a vast, cold space, the high walls lined with ancient tapestries and armor of the Fireborn warriors. At the far end of the room, the Fireborn king sat on his throne, his eyes dark and calculating, watching them approach with an unreadable expression.

"Aeryn," the Fireborn king's voice rang out, cold and commanding. "You return at last. I trust you've come to your senses."

Aeryn's hands tightened into fists at her sides, the fire inside her surging to life. She fought to keep it under control, but it burned hotter the closer she got to him. The truth of what he had done—what he had turned her into—was unbearable. The man who had once been her father, the one she had tried so hard to please, now felt like a stranger.

"I've come to stop this," Aeryn said, her voice steady, but beneath it lay a tremor of uncertainty. "I'm not going to help you wage war on the Iceborn, Father."

The king's expression didn't change. His eyes, as cold and fiery as the kingdom they ruled, were fixed on her, unblinking. "You think you have a choice in the matter, Aeryn? You are Fireborn. Your blood is my blood. You were born for this."

"I was born to bring peace," she replied, her voice firm despite the rising heat in her chest. "Not destruction."

Her father's lips curled into a thin smile, one that sent a chill through Aeryn's bones. "Peace?" he echoed, his voice laced with sarcasm. "There is no peace for the Fireborn, Aeryn. You know that. There never has been."

Thorne stepped forward, his body tense, his presence like an icy gust that chilled the air around them. "The prophecy is a curse, not a destiny," he said, his voice low but sharp. "We don't have to follow it. We don't have to become your tools."

The king's eyes flicked to Thorne, narrowing with a predatory gleam. "Ah, the Iceborn prince," he said, his tone dripping with disdain. "You think your power can protect her? You think you can protect her from what she is?"

Aeryn felt a flash of fear at his words, but she refused to let it show. She could feel the fire inside her surging, responding to her father's presence, to the danger that loomed in the air. The temperature in the room rose, the flames in her chest growing hotter, stronger.

"I won't be your weapon," she said through clenched teeth, her fists trembling at her sides.

The king stood, his towering figure looming over them. "You don't have a choice, Aeryn. You're mine. You always have been."

With a sudden, terrifying movement, the king extended his hand, and the room seemed to shake with the force of his power. The flames in the room flared, licking at the stone walls, the heat intensifying. Aeryn could feel the pressure of it, the weight of the fire pushing against her like a physical force.

Thorne's voice broke through the heat, his words barely audible over the roar of the fire. "Aeryn, get back!"

But it was too late. The fire surged, and with a violent explosion, the heat overwhelmed her. Aeryn felt her power explode outward, the flames erupting from her in a wave of intense heat, blasting back at the Fireborn king. The sheer force of it knocked him off his feet, sending him sprawling backward toward his throne.

Thorne moved instinctively, stepping forward to shield her from the blast. His icy power surged to life, an explosion of cold that clashed with her flames, creating a wall of steam between them and the king. The room was filled with a deafening roar as the two forces collided, fire and ice battling for control.

"Thorne, no!" Aeryn shouted, but it was too late. His ice—his fury—had already unleashed itself.

In that instant, everything changed.

The temperature in the room plummeted, freezing the air around them in an instant. The flames that had once been a part of Aeryn's body were now fighting against the icy storm that Thorne had summoned. Steam poured from the collision of fire and ice, filling the room with a blinding haze. The world seemed to spin, the elements clashing around them, threatening to tear the very palace apart.

Aeryn could feel the energy spiraling out of control, her power roaring inside her like a beast that could no longer be contained. She reached out to Thorne, her heart pounding, but the cold of his powers pushed her back, his anger and fear feeding the storm around them.

"Thorne!" she cried again, her voice desperate.

But his icy fury only intensified. He was no longer just trying to protect her—he was fighting to control the rage that had built up inside him, the fear of losing her, the fear of the prophecy becoming real.

The king's laughter broke through the chaos, cruel and triumphant. "You think you can stop it? You think you can stop me? You are nothing but children playing at war, trying to defy fate."

Aeryn's heart stopped. **Children.** That's how he saw them. A weapon to be wielded, a tool to be used.

The king extended his hand again, but this time, the flames didn't come from him. They surged from the walls themselves, as though the very palace was alive with fire, angry and vengeful. The flames leaped at them, a torrent of heat that threatened to consume everything in its path.

Thorne's ice crashed against it, but the heat was overwhelming. He stumbled backward, his strength faltering as the flames burned hotter, pushing him to his knees.

"No!" Aeryn screamed, her voice desperate as she reached out to him.

But the flames were too much. Her fire was at its limit, the power inside her struggling against the ice that Thorne was unleashing. The two forces, once so perfectly balanced, now felt like an unsolvable riddle, each trying to dominate the other.

She was losing him, losing control, and she didn't know how to stop it.

The room seemed to collapse around them, the fire and ice swirling in a chaotic frenzy, the palace shaking as if it were being torn apart from the inside.

Aeryn's chest tightened with fear, with guilt, with the knowledge that everything they had fought for was slipping away. The prophecy was becoming real. And there was nothing they could do to stop it.

Thorne's eyes locked with hers through the haze of steam and flame. There was something broken in his gaze—something he had never shown her before. **Fear.**

"I can't control it anymore," he whispered, his voice filled with pain. "I can't stop it, Aeryn."

"I don't want to fight you," she said, her voice thick with tears. "I don't want to lose you."

The heat and cold were suffocating, their powers clashing in an endless struggle for dominance. And in that moment, Aeryn realized the truth—no matter how much she tried to fight it, no matter how much she loved him, there was a cost to their love. The prophecy demanded it.

Aeryn's heart shattered as the power within her surged once again, and she screamed, her voice breaking through the chaos. She didn't know how much longer she could hold on.

But Thorne, his icy resolve faltering, reached out for her, his touch the only thing she could hold onto. In that moment, they were no longer just fire and ice. They were something more—something that could either save them or destroy them.

And the world around them trembled, unsure of which would come first.

Together or apart?

They had no choice but to face it.

Aeryn's heart thundered in her chest, her pulse racing as she reached for Thorne, her hand trembling with desperation. The world around them seemed to shudder with every clash of fire and ice, the palace groaning under the weight of the elemental forces that fought against each other. The air was thick with heat, freezing cold, and steam, blurring everything in a haze of chaos. The ground beneath their feet cracked and split, the very foundation of the palace trembling as if it were about to collapse into ruin.

Thorne's gaze met hers—filled with pain, filled with fear— and for a moment, she saw the man she had fallen in love with. The ice around him was not just his power; it was his fear, his insecurities, his desire to protect her from the very thing he had always feared becoming: a weapon, a force that could destroy everything. She had seen that fear before, but never like this. It was consuming him now, and she could feel it in the way the air around them chilled with the force of his powers.

Aeryn stepped forward, her fire burning brighter as she closed the distance between them. "Thorne, please," she pleaded, her voice cracking. "We're stronger than this! We're stronger than the prophecy. We don't have to let it tear us apart."

But his eyes darkened, his breath coming in sharp bursts as he struggled to keep his powers in check. He couldn't stop the cold that had become an extension of him. It was as much a part of him as the fire that roared within her.

"I'm trying, Aeryn," Thorne gritted out, his voice strained. "I'm trying to stop it, but it's too much. I can't control it anymore. The more I fight, the worse it gets. I can feel it slipping. I'm afraid of what I might do. What I'll *become*."

The ice in the air intensified, whipping around them, like a storm that was threatening to consume everything. The palace walls groaned under the weight of their powers, the fire roaring in response to Thorne's chilling fury. Aeryn could feel her own fire struggling against the ice, both of them locked in an eternal tug-of-war. The friction between them was unbearable. It felt as though her flames were being smothered, her soul suffocating beneath the icy grip of Thorne's emotions.

"I won't let you do this alone, Thorne," she said, her voice firm but trembling. "I'm here. Please, let me help you."

He flinched, his eyes flickering with something that might have been regret, but it was quickly buried beneath the storm that raged inside him.

"You can't," he whispered, his voice so soft, it was barely audible over the chaos. "I'm not the man you thought I was, Aeryn. I'm not the man who can save you. I'm the one who will destroy everything."

Tears pricked at the corners of her eyes, but she refused to let them fall. The heat in her chest surged with a force she could barely control, but she clenched her fists, willing it to remain contained. She couldn't afford to lose control again—not now.

"You're wrong," she said fiercely. "You've always been more than just your powers, Thorne. You're the one who saved me. You're the one who helped me fight my fears. Don't let this break you. We can still fight this. Together."

The storm around them seemed to pause for a split second, a brief moment of stillness in the eye of the tempest. Thorne's breath hitched, his chest rising and falling rapidly as if he were trying to hold onto something that was slipping away. The ice around him shimmered, crackling with the intensity of his internal battle, but still, he didn't reach for her.

The king, watching from his throne, now stood, his expression one of smug satisfaction. The air in the room grew warmer, his firepower flaring with malicious intent. "Pathetic," he sneered, his voice dripping with disdain. "You're both fools, thinking you can defy fate. I warned you, Aeryn. Your bloodline is cursed. You were born to serve the fire, but also to destroy it. And he," the king said, gesturing toward Thorne, "is nothing but a threat that needs to be extinguished."

Aeryn's heart skipped a beat. **Her father**, standing in the distance, had always viewed her as an instrument of war, but now he was playing his hand, testing the very limits of their abilities. He had been using her all along, manipulating the prophecy as if it were a game. The weight of his cruelty hit her like a physical blow, but she refused to let it show. She could feel the fire inside her thrumming with fury, with the realization that everything she had been taught, everything she had fought for, had been a lie. Her own father had planned to use her, to burn everything down.

"No," Aeryn said, her voice rising, filled with conviction. "I won't be your weapon, Father. I won't let you destroy everything. Not now. Not ever."

The king's expression darkened, his lips curling into a sinister smile. "You have no choice," he said coldly. "You will burn, Aeryn. And so will he."

Before Aeryn could react, the king raised his hand, and with it, a wave of fire exploded from his palm, streaking toward her with blinding speed. Thorne's reaction was instinctive. He moved faster than she could blink, stepping in front of her and unleashing his ice to intercept the flames. The two elements collided with a deafening crash, the heat and cold battling in the air with a force that shook the palace to its core.

Aeryn gasped, the blast sending shockwaves through her body, knocking her back a few steps. The room around them trembled, cracks appearing in the stone walls as the clash between fire and ice reached catastrophic levels.

"Thorne!" Aeryn screamed, rushing to him as he struggled to stay upright, his ice powers faltering under the intensity of the heat.

His face was pale, his breath coming in ragged gasps, but his eyes were filled with determination. "Get back!" he shouted at her, his voice strained. "I can't hold this much longer."

The king stepped forward, his smirk widening as he watched the destruction unfold. The flames licked at the edges of the room, filling it with a suffocating heat. Aeryn could feel her own fire burning with an uncontrollable rage, but she didn't know how to stop it. The room was filled with a swirling chaos, her flames battling Thorne's ice, her father's fire searing the very air around them. It was all becoming too much.

Thorne's icy power flickered one last time, his strength giving out under the weight of the attack. He collapsed to his knees, his ice cracking and shattering as the fire overwhelmed him. Aeryn cried out, reaching for him, but the flames pushed her back, forcing her to stumble and fall to the ground.

"Thorne!" she shouted, her voice hoarse with desperation.

The king laughed, his eyes glowing with twisted amusement. "It's over, Aeryn. You've failed. Your love for him will be your downfall."

Aeryn's chest tightened, but she refused to let the fear take over. She couldn't lose him. Not like this.

She staggered to her feet, summoning every ounce of her power. Her fire surged again, but this time, it wasn't just the heat of her anger. It was something deeper, something that had been brewing inside her ever since she had made the choice to follow Thorne. Her flames wrapped around her, hotter, fiercer, alive with the desperate need to protect him.

The Fireborn king's laughter faltered as he saw her stand, the intensity of her power growing. "You think you can stop me?" he sneered.

"I think I can stop you," Aeryn said, her voice low but filled with unshakable determination. "And I will."

With a force that shook the very foundation of the palace, Aeryn unleashed her flames, not at the king, but at the walls around them. The fire spread like a tidal wave, consuming the room in a brilliant, blinding blaze. The heat, the power, the fury of everything she had felt—the betrayal, the fear, the love—was released in a single, devastating surge.

The king's fire faltered in the face of her power, his flames flickering and dying as the heat of Aeryn's blaze engulfed everything in its path. The room began to crack, the stone walls collapsing under the intensity of the fire and ice clashing together.

"NO!" the king screamed, his voice breaking as he tried to retreat, but it was too late. The fire had already consumed him, and with one final, violent explosion, the palace was reduced to ruins.

Aeryn fell to her knees, her flames fading into embers as the world around her crumbled. Thorne was beside her, his body weak and trembling, but he was still alive. She reached for him, her hand trembling as she touched his cold skin.

"I'm sorry," she whispered, her voice filled with guilt and love. "I never wanted this. I never wanted to hurt you."

Thorne's eyes opened, his gaze locking onto hers, but the

coldness had not fully receded. "We have to decide, Aeryn," he said, his voice rough. "Together or apart."

Aeryn felt her heart break in her chest. She knew what the answer had to be, but the cost of that choice, of their love, was something they would both have to bear.

The choice wasn't just about them anymore. It was about the fate of their worlds.

And in the smoldering ruins of the palace, Aeryn and Thorne faced the future—one that could either destroy them both or bind them together forever.

Together. Or apart.

Eleven

The Heart of the Storm

The storm had come without warning.

Aeryn could feel it in the air long before she saw the dark clouds swirling on the horizon, their ominous shapes bending and twisting as though alive. The wind picked up, howling through the trees with a ferocity that made the very earth tremble beneath her feet. The fire within her flickered, an unsettling warmth that hummed with an undercurrent of fear. Thorne was beside her, his icy presence colder than ever, but even he seemed to sense the impending danger. His expression was unreadable, his eyes scanning the horizon with a calmness that betrayed the tension in his body. He was ready—ready to fight, but for what? For whom?

The peace they had fought for was slipping through their fingers, slipping into the darkness that now loomed over them.

"Aeryn," Thorne's voice broke through her thoughts, low and tense. "It's here."

She nodded, her heart sinking as she turned to face the storm. It was not just a storm. It was something worse—something unnatural, a force of nature that pulsed with an energy she couldn't explain. The winds were a violent maelstrom, whipping across the landscape with blinding speed, and the air seemed to crackle with an electric charge that made her skin crawl.

"We have to move," Aeryn said, her voice tight, trying to ignore the fear that gnawed at her. "It's coming straight for us."

Thorne's gaze hardened as he glanced back at the darkening sky. "No," he replied quietly. "It's coming for us all."

Aeryn's breath caught in her throat. The weight of his words pressed down on her like a lead weight. The storm was not just nature at its worst. It was deliberate—an attack. An assault. And it wasn't just the wind and the rain that threatened them. No. There was something more. Something worse.

The sky split open with a deafening roar, the first wave of the storm crashing down upon them. The earth shook, the ground splintering as bolts of lightning arced through the sky, striking the earth with devastating force. Aeryn had to brace herself against the violent gusts of wind, her fiery power flickering at the edge of her control, trying to resist the overwhelming surge of energy that threatened to drown her.

And then she saw it—a figure standing at the center of the storm, emerging from the chaos like a shadow. A figure that sent a chill through her body, colder than anything Thorne could conjure.

The figure was cloaked in shadows, its form shifting and swirling with the storm. Its eyes gleamed with a terrible light, bright and cruel, burning with an unnatural intensity. It was like nothing Aeryn had ever seen before, a being of pure chaos, its very presence distorting the world around it.

Aeryn's heart raced, her fire sparking to life in an instant. But the figure didn't flinch. It stood there, calm and unyielding, as if it were the storm itself, its power drawing from the chaos it had created. Aeryn knew, without a doubt, that this was no ordinary foe. This was something far worse.

Thorne stepped forward, his icy presence like a shield in front of her. The air around him crackled with cold, but even his strength seemed to falter against the force of the storm. The lightning in the sky turned from blue to a sickly green, crackling with an unnatural energy that made Aeryn's fire flicker and burn brighter.

"It's not just the storm," Aeryn whispered, her eyes locked onto the figure. "It's him. This is the enemy. The one we've been warned about."

Thorne nodded grimly, his icy eyes narrowing. "The one who can control both fire and ice. The one who was supposed to be a legend. A ghost."

The figure stepped closer, its movements fluid and unnerving. Aeryn's heart pounded, the air around them heavy with the crushing weight of its power. The figure's voice was like the wind itself, a low and hollow whisper that seemed to come from all directions at once.

"You should have known, Fireborn," the figure spoke, its voice cold and empty. "You cannot control the storm. You cannot defeat the one who is both fire and ice."

Aeryn's blood ran cold. "What do you want?" she demanded, her voice shaking despite her best efforts to remain calm.

"What I've always wanted," the figure said, its form shifting in the wind, its eyes glowing with a terrifying light. "To be whole. To bring about the end of the world you know. To break the bond between fire and ice."

Thorne stepped forward, his body tense with barely contained rage. "You'll never win. We'll stop you."

The figure's laugh was low and mocking. "You are nothing but children playing at war. You are the last hope, but you will not survive. Fire and ice were never meant to be together. You are the greatest threat to your own worlds."

Aeryn's heart pounded in her chest. The prophecy. The figure before them was the one the prophecy had warned them about—the one who could harness both fire and ice. And now, they were standing at the heart of the storm, facing the very creature that threatened to destroy everything they had fought for.

"You're wrong," Aeryn said, her voice rising with the intensity of the heat inside her. "We won't let you destroy us. We'll fight."

The figure's eyes glowed brighter, its power swirling around them like an unstoppable force. The winds picked up again, the chaos around them intensifying.

Thorne stepped forward, his ice powers flaring as he unleashed a blast of freezing energy, the cold surging toward the figure with devastating force. But the figure raised a hand, and the air around them seemed to distort, rippling like water.

The ice shattered into nothingness, consumed by the storm.

Aeryn gasped, her heart sinking. This wasn't just any foe. This was something beyond their power. But they couldn't stop now. She wouldn't let it win.

"I won't let you take him," she said fiercely, her fire blazing brighter as she summoned every ounce of her power. The heat surged from her, a wave of flames that roared and crackled with fury. The figure's storm twisted in response, clashing against her fire, but she pushed forward, determined to fight.

Thorne's ice followed, his cold presence moving to reinforce her, to shield her from the chaos. The two of them, fire and ice, were no longer just two opposing forces. They were one. They had become a single, unstoppable entity, their powers merging and clashing, building into a devastating storm of their own.

The figure in the center of the chaos recoiled for a moment, a flicker of surprise crossing its face. But it quickly regained its composure, its smile twisting into something far more sinister.

"You think you can stop me with your petty flames and ice?" the figure hissed, its voice growing louder, more guttural. "You are nothing. You are the children of a dying world."

The winds howled, and the figure raised both hands, the storm around them intensifying to a deafening roar. The ground beneath their feet cracked, the very air distorting with the force of its power.

Thorne's eyes burned with ice, but he didn't flinch. Aeryn's heart raced in her chest, her fire burning hotter, fiercer, until it felt like the very air around them was burning. She could feel the bond between her and Thorne strengthening—every pulse of her fire synchronizing with his cold fury, creating a force that could either save or destroy them.

"We are more than what you think," Aeryn shouted, her voice rising above the chaos. "We are *together*. Fire and ice, together. And we will stop you."

The figure's eyes narrowed, its grin widening with cruel satisfaction. "We shall see," it sneered.

With a flick of its hand, the storm intensified, and a wall of lightning surged toward them, crackling with deadly energy. Aeryn braced herself, but before she could react, Thorne's ice surged forward, a wall of freezing power that collided with the storm, halting it in its tracks. The lightning arced against the ice, sizzling with unbearable heat, and Aeryn followed with a burst of fire, turning the heat into a conflagration that burned brighter than the sun itself.

The figure faltered, but it was only for a moment. The storm around them howled again, more violent than before, and Aeryn realized they were reaching their limit. The energy between them—the fire and the ice—was growing too intense, too unstable. They couldn't keep this up for long.

"Thorne," Aeryn shouted over the roar of the storm. "We have to combine our powers—*now*. If we don't, we'll both burn out."

Thorne's eyes met hers, his expression conflicted, but he nodded, stepping closer, the ice swirling around him like a shield. Aeryn felt the heat in her chest surge, her flames burning brighter as she reached out for him, their powers connecting in an explosion of energy that lit up the entire sky.

The storm around them began to buckle under the force of their combined power, fire and ice merging in a cataclysmic explosion. For a brief moment, time seemed to stand still, the world holding its breath as the battle raged around them.

And then, with a final surge of power, they unleashed everything they had. The storm roared in fury, but it was nothing compared to the force of their combined fury. The blast of fire and ice tore through the figure's storm, shattering it with a deafening crash that echoed across the kingdom.

The figure screamed in fury, its form dissipating in the chaos of their combined force, leaving only the silence that followed.

Aeryn and Thorne stood, their bodies trembling with the aftermath, their powers flickering weakly as the storm finally subsided. The air around them was still, the winds dying down, leaving only the quiet hum of their power in the aftermath.

But it wasn't over.

They had won, yes, but the cost was clear. The bond between them was stronger than ever, but the strain of what they had just done had left them both exhausted, their bodies trembling with the weight of the battle they had fought.

Aeryn looked at Thorne, her heart racing, but as their eyes met, she saw something new in his gaze—something deeper than before. They had faced the storm together. They had become the storm.

And now, standing in the aftermath, they knew the hardest part was yet to come.

Their love had survived this battle. But what would it cost them next?

The air was thick with the lingering aftermath of their struggle, the oppressive silence that followed the storm almost as deafening as the chaos that had come before it. Aeryn could feel the remnants of her fire still smoldering deep within her, flickering weakly, and Thorne's icy presence, though dimmed, still clung to the air around them like a frozen breath. Their bodies were sore from the battle, and the weight of exhaustion hung heavy on them both. Yet, despite the battle they had just faced, the storm that had threatened to tear them apart, there was something else in the air now. Something more… ominous.

Aeryn could sense it—the quiet before the next storm. The battle was over, but the war had only just begun.

She turned to Thorne, meeting his gaze as they stood in the now-ruined throne room, the palace itself cracked and crumbling around them. The walls, once strong and proud, now seemed like fragile remnants of an era long past. The power they had unleashed had shattered more than just the storm; it had destroyed the very foundation of their world.

Thorne's eyes were still clouded with the aftershocks of the battle, the ice that had once been his shield now feeling like a burden that weighed him down. His breath was shallow, but there was something in his gaze—a flicker of determination mixed with something darker, something fearful.

"Did we win?" he asked, his voice hoarse, barely above a whisper.

Aeryn's heart twisted as she saw the vulnerability in him, the rawness beneath the cool, collected exterior. They had fought together—fought with every ounce of their power, with everything they had. But the toll had been great.

"We stopped him," she said softly, her own voice strained. "But I don't think it's over, Thorne. This was only a part of it."

Thorne's gaze shifted to the shattered remnants of the room. His shoulders tensed, the weight of his powers still a heavy presence around him. "What do you mean?"

Aeryn glanced around, her mind working furiously to process what had just happened. The storm had been powerful, yes, but it had been manipulated, twisted into something greater by the figure they had faced. The figure—who had claimed to be the force that controlled both fire and ice—wasn't just an anomaly. It had been a force trying to break them apart, trying to destroy their bond, their very connection.

"Whoever—or *whatever*—that thing was, it's not the only one. There are more," Aeryn said, her voice steady despite the rising tide of panic inside her. "And they're not going to stop until they've destroyed everything."

Thorne's eyes narrowed, the cold resolve returning to his gaze. But it wasn't just ice now. There was something else

there—a burning need to protect, to defend. To stand by her, even when the world seemed intent on tearing them apart.

"We've been used," he said bitterly, his voice filled with the weight of realization. "Not just by your father, but by whoever is behind all this. They're using our power, Aeryn. The prophecy… it wasn't just about us. It was about what we could destroy."

Aeryn swallowed hard, the implications of his words sinking in like a blade in her gut. She had known, deep down, that the prophecy wasn't just about her. About Thorne. It had been designed to use them, to manipulate their strengths and weaknesses against each other, to destroy the balance between them.

"That's why they've kept us apart," Aeryn whispered. "Why we were pushed into conflict. They needed us to break… so they could control what was left of our power."

Thorne clenched his fists at his sides, his breath coming in sharp, ragged gasps. The cold, once his comfort, now felt like an encroaching storm. "But we've fought it. Together."

Aeryn took a step toward him, her hand reaching out, but he didn't move. The distance between them was widening again, not just physically, but emotionally, as the gravity of everything they had just faced began to settle in. They had defeated the storm, but the battle was far from over. The real enemy still loomed, and with it, the fear that they might not be enough.

She reached for him again, her fingers brushing the edge of his arm, a gentle touch that was more a plea than a command. "Thorne, we can do this. We have to. Together."

His gaze flickered, uncertainty swirling in the cold depths of his eyes. But then, he softened, just slightly, the walls he had built around himself lowering for a moment. "You're right," he said quietly, his voice thick with a mix of pain and determination. "We've been through too much already to let them win now."

Aeryn's heart fluttered with a mixture of hope and fear. The bond between them, fragile as it was, had been forged in fire and ice. They had faced impossible odds together. But the storm they had just weathered was only a shadow of the storm to come. And now, she feared the real battle was not against an external enemy. It was within themselves.

Before she could speak again, the ground trembled beneath them, the palace vibrating with a power that came from deep within the earth itself. The walls creaked, the stone groaning as though the entire structure was about to collapse. Aeryn's heart lurched. **It's not over.**

Thorne's icy powers surged instinctively, but the coldness didn't protect them from the danger that was closing in. The storm outside—the real storm—had returned, stronger than before, and this time, it was not just a battle of forces. It was a battle of wills, of destinies colliding with all-consuming force.

Aeryn felt the fire inside her stir again, but it wasn't just the flicker of her power. It was the truth—the realization that she and Thorne, together, were more than just fire and ice. They were the balance between them. And if they failed to understand that, if they failed to embrace both their strengths and weaknesses, they would destroy everything.

"I'm not ready for this," Aeryn whispered, her voice shaking. "Thorne, I—"

"You are," Thorne interrupted, his voice firm, but his own fear was evident in the way his shoulders tensed. He wasn't just speaking to her. He was speaking to himself. To them both.

The world shook around them, and the walls cracked further, but Aeryn didn't look away from him. She could see it now—see the truth that had always been there. They weren't just two people struggling to survive a prophecy. They were the key. Together, they held the power to destroy or protect the world. It was their love—this impossible bond—that was their true weapon. And it was up to them to wield it, no matter the cost.

Thorne reached for her, his icy fingers touching hers with a warmth that seemed out of place, a flicker of something human in the frozen chaos. His eyes softened, and for the first time, Aeryn saw him not as the man who feared his own power, but as the man who needed her as much as she needed him.

"We're not alone in this," he said softly. "I won't let you go. Not now. Not ever."

The storm outside raged, but Aeryn felt a new surge of fire within her, fueled by the strength of their bond. She wasn't just fighting for herself anymore. She was fighting for them—for the future they could still create together. If they could survive the storm within themselves, they would survive the storm outside.

She squeezed his hand, feeling the warmth of his touch against the cold of his powers, a symbol of the fragile, yet unyielding connection they shared.

"We can face this," she said, her voice steady, filled with the fire of determination. "Together."

And just as the final remnants of the storm gathered, building to a cataclysmic crescendo, Aeryn and Thorne stood side by side, their powers ready to combine in a force that was greater than either fire or ice alone.

They had come this far, and no matter what the storm would

throw at them, they would face it head-on.

Together.

The world shook around them as the storm converged, and the battle for their worlds began in earnest.

Twelve

The Hidden Truth

The sun had barely begun to rise over the shattered remains of the Fireborn palace, casting long shadows across the snow-laden ground. The storm that had ravaged the land the night before had passed, but the air still hummed with tension, the sky clouded with an uneasy stillness. Aeryn stood on the edge of the ruins, her eyes scanning the horizon as she felt the weight of the world pressing in on her. The calm after the storm was deceiving, and the aftermath of their battle was far from over. She had seen the devastation the storm had caused, not just to the palace, but to the very hearts of those who had fought within its walls. It was not just the physical destruction they now faced; it was the toll it had taken on their spirits.

Her gaze turned to Thorne, who stood a few paces behind her, his silhouette sharp against the backdrop of the destroyed kingdom. His figure was as imposing as ever, but there was a darkness about him now, a heaviness that had settled in his chest, one she hadn't seen before.

Aeryn felt it too, the silence between them, the growing distance that had come after their last confrontation. They had fought side by side, but the aftermath had left scars neither of them knew how to heal.

"Thorne," she called softly, her voice barely above a whisper, carried by the faint breeze. She turned to face him as he slowly walked toward her, his boots crunching in the snow with each step. The cold that radiated from him seemed to pull the warmth from the air around them, a reminder of the battle they'd fought and the one still to come.

He met her gaze, and for the briefest moment, she saw the conflict in his eyes—the uncertainty, the storm of emotions that churned beneath the surface. He didn't speak right away, and the silence stretched between them, thick with the unsaid words, the unacknowledged fears.

"I don't know if I can do this," Thorne said, his voice low, his breath visible in the cold air. "Not anymore."

Aeryn's heart clenched at the sound of his words. She had known something was off, had felt the shift in the energy between them since the storm. But hearing it spoken aloud felt like a knife twisting in her gut.

"You don't have to do this alone," she said, stepping closer, her hand reaching out to him. "We're in this together, Thorne. We always have been."

His eyes flickered with a mixture of pain and doubt. He stepped back, his posture rigid, the distance between them growing once more. "Aeryn," he began, his voice strained, "there's something I haven't told you. Something that I've been keeping from you."

Her heart skipped, her hand falling to her side. "What do you mean?"

Thorne took a deep breath, his eyes narrowing as though bracing for a storm far greater than the one they had just weathered. "I'm not just the son of an Iceborn king, Aeryn. There's more to this… more to me than I ever knew."

Aeryn's confusion deepened. The words hung in the air between them, as though they carried a weight she couldn't understand, a burden that only he could bear. "What are you saying, Thorne?"

He turned away, his back to her as he looked out toward the ruined kingdom. The air around them crackled with the remnants of their battle, and Aeryn could feel the tension building, a quiet storm on the horizon. "I've spent my life running from my legacy, from the expectations of my father, of my people. But I've never been just his son. I've never been just an Iceborn prince. The truth is… I'm part of the prophecy."

The words struck Aeryn like a bolt of lightning. She couldn't breathe for a moment, her chest tight as the implications of his revelation began to sink in. The prophecy. The ancient words that had foretold the destruction of both kingdoms, that had twisted their fates together in a way neither of them could escape. The very prophecy that had haunted her since the day she was born.

"No," Aeryn whispered, her voice shaky. "You can't mean—"

Thorne turned to face her then, his eyes filled with pain, the coldness in his gaze more pronounced than ever before. "I do mean it. I don't know all of it yet, but I know enough. My blood—our blood—is tied to the prophecy. I'm not just meant to destroy the Iceborn. I'm meant to unite both kingdoms, Aeryn. And that union…" His voice faltered for a moment.

"That union was always meant to bring both fire and ice together. It was never supposed to be a bond of love. It was supposed to be a bond of war."

Aeryn felt the world tilt beneath her feet. She took a step back, her hands trembling as she processed his words. The prophecy, the one that had bound their lives together in ways neither of them could fully understand, was now more than just a distant threat. It was part of Thorne's bloodline, part of who he was—and it had been all along.

Thorne stepped closer to her, his expression tormented. "I didn't know, Aeryn. I never asked for this. But it's there. And now… now I don't know what to do. I don't know if I can be the man you need me to be. If I can be the man I thought I was."

Aeryn swallowed hard, her mind racing. She had spent her life trying to escape the prophecy, trying to defy the destiny that had been thrust upon her, and now, Thorne was telling her that the prophecy was not just something that had bound them together—it had shaped who they were, who they were meant to be. And worse, it was pulling them toward something neither of them could control.

Her heart ached as she looked at him, the raw vulnerability in his eyes. He was lost, torn between the man he had always been and the fate that awaited him. He wasn't just afraid of the prophecy—he was afraid of becoming the very thing he had always feared.

Aeryn stepped toward him, her heart heavy. "Thorne," she said softly, her voice cracking with emotion. "I don't care what the prophecy says. I don't care what it's meant to be. We are *more* than this. We're *together*, and that's what matters."

Thorne's expression twisted with grief, and he turned away

from her, his body tense with the weight of his thoughts. "You don't understand, Aeryn," he said, his voice low. "It's not just about us. It's about *everything*. The prophecy says one of us must die, one of us must bring balance by sacrificing the other. And I can't… I can't live with that."

Aeryn felt her chest tighten. She took a deep breath, her hand trembling as she reached for him. "Thorne, no. We can fight this. We can fight the prophecy. Together."

Thorne's eyes burned with cold fire. "But I don't know if I can. What if I'm the one who has to die? What if you're the one who has to choose?"

Aeryn froze, her heart plummeting at the thought. She had never considered that—never thought that the prophecy might require them to choose between each other. The very idea twisted her insides, turning her thoughts into a storm of confusion.

"Don't say that," she whispered, her voice breaking. "We won't let it come to that."

But the weight of his words had already set in, the truth of their situation beginning to settle in the pit of her stomach. She could feel the storm of emotions inside her, the fierce pull of their bond, but also the fear that it might not be enough. Not to survive the prophecy. Not to survive what was coming for them.

They stood there for a long moment, the cold wind tugging at their clothes, the ruins of the palace standing silent behind them. Aeryn's mind raced, her heart torn between love and duty. Could she truly stand by him, knowing that the prophecy would demand a sacrifice? Could she risk everything for the chance at a life together, when the cost of that life might be too great?

Thorne's voice cut through her thoughts, raw and broken. "I'm afraid, Aeryn. Afraid of what I might become. Afraid of what I might have to do to protect you. To protect us."

She reached for him, her hand trembling as she placed it on his arm. "You don't have to do this alone, Thorne. We'll figure it out. Together."

His eyes locked onto hers, and for a moment, the world around them seemed to fade away. It was just them—their hearts, their bond, their love. She could feel the weight of the prophecy pressing in on them, but it didn't matter. Not now.

"Together," he whispered, his voice thick with emotion.

But even as the words left his lips, Aeryn knew they were standing at a crossroads. The choice was no longer just about the prophecy—it was about the future of their love. Could they face it together, knowing that the cost could be their very lives?

The storm was coming. And whether they survived it depended on the choice they made now.

Aeryn looked into Thorne's eyes, her heart racing with fear and hope, and knew that whatever choice they made, it would change everything.

The wind howled through the broken palace walls, a constant reminder of the tempest that raged not just outside, but within them both. Aeryn stood in the midst of it, her body trembling not just from the cold, but from the weight of Thorne's words. The prophecy had always loomed over them like a shadow, but now it was something tangible, something they could no longer ignore. She could feel it—feel the weight of it pressing down on them both, shaping the path before them.

Thorne's eyes, filled with an intensity she had never seen

before, held hers with a mixture of fear and something darker—something that seemed to twist in his chest. He was afraid, she knew that much. But so was she. Fear had become a constant companion, a shadow at their backs, whispering doubts and uncertainties in their ears.

"I can't do this, Aeryn," Thorne's voice was strained, the words heavy, as if each one cost him something. He turned away from her, his fists clenched at his sides, the cold radiating from him like a wall. "I don't know if I can be the man you need me to be. I don't even know if I can be the man I was before all this. The prophecy… it's part of me. It's in my blood. And I can't escape it."

Aeryn took a deep breath, her chest tight, her thoughts swirling in a storm of confusion. She could feel the fire inside her, pulsing with the need to reach out to him, to pull him back from the edge. But the fear that gripped her heart held her in place. The love she felt for him was fierce, unyielding, but the reality of the prophecy—the promise of destruction that hovered above them—was more than she could bear.

"You don't have to be anyone other than who you are," Aeryn said, her voice cracking as she stepped closer to him. She reached for his arm, her fingers trembling against his cold skin. "Thorne, you're not your bloodline. You're not your past. You're the man who stood beside me when everything seemed lost. You're the one who fought for us."

Thorne's eyes flickered with something—perhaps hope, perhaps doubt—but he didn't look at her. His gaze was fixed on the remnants of the kingdom they had once known, his thoughts clearly miles away from her, lost in the dark depths of his mind.

"You don't understand," he muttered, his voice distant. "I

was never meant to be this—this man who stands between two worlds. The prophecy was never just about us. It's about the future of both kingdoms. And I'm part of that fate. If I don't make the right choice, Aeryn… if I don't accept what I am, it will destroy everything we've fought for. And you'll be the one to pay the price."

The air between them grew colder, if that was even possible. Aeryn could feel the icy tendrils of his power creeping in, the coldness that had always been a part of him now spreading like an insidious disease. His words, the weight of them, crushed her chest. She had always known the prophecy would come for them, but hearing him say it out loud, hearing him voice the fear that had always been in the back of her mind, made everything feel so real, so final.

She stepped forward, her fingers still resting on his arm, and for the first time in what felt like an eternity, Thorne allowed her to hold him. His body was tense, stiff with fear, but he didn't pull away.

"You don't have to make that choice alone," Aeryn said softly, her voice shaking. "We can face it together. Whatever happens, we do this together. You've always been more than your powers, Thorne. I know you. I *believe* in you."

His eyes, cold and stormy, met hers, and for a moment, she saw the man he had once been. The man who had fought for her, who had trusted her with his heart. But that man was slipping away, and she felt powerless to stop it.

"Do you really believe that?" Thorne asked, his voice so raw that it felt like it was breaking apart. "Can you truly believe in a man who is bound to a fate that will destroy everything? I can't protect you from that, Aeryn. I can't protect us."

Aeryn's heart ached at the desperation in his voice. She

stepped closer, her chest against his, the warmth of her fire against the cold of his ice. She could feel him shudder beneath her touch, his body trembling with the weight of his fears, but she didn't pull away. She held on, as if holding him in her arms could hold back the storm that threatened to tear them apart.

"I believe in us, Thorne," she whispered, her voice steady now. "I believe that together, we can face anything. Even the prophecy."

For a long time, Thorne didn't respond. He stood still, his breath shallow as he stared at her, as if searching for something in her eyes—something he hadn't seen before. Aeryn could feel his icy resolve begin to crack, piece by piece, but it wasn't enough. Not yet. The storm inside him was still raging.

"Do you really think we can change this?" Thorne asked quietly, his voice laced with doubt. "Do you really think we can fight the prophecy?"

Aeryn didn't hesitate. She had to make him see it—had to make him understand that their love, their bond, was stronger than the fate they were supposed to follow.

"I don't think we can *change* the prophecy," she said, her voice fierce. "But we can *choose* how we face it. And we choose together. If you die, I die, Thorne. And if I die, you die. We're bound to each other. Our fates are tied."

Thorne's eyes softened, his gaze shifting from cold to something warmer, something that flickered with the remnants of the man she had once known. His lips parted as if he wanted to say something, but the words never came. Instead, he reached for her, his icy hand brushing against her skin. The touch sent a shock through her, but it was a shock that wasn't just cold—it was something more. A warmth began to build between them, a force greater than either fire or ice.

Aeryn felt the pulse of power that connected them, the pull of the prophecy, the weight of their destinies colliding. She had known from the beginning that this moment would come. But now, standing in front of Thorne, her heart beating in time with his, she realized something else—something that terrified her more than anything else.

This battle, the one for their love, was not one that could be won with fire or ice. It would take something far greater.

"I can't let you go," she whispered, her voice thick with emotion. "I won't."

Thorne stared at her for a long moment, his gaze searching hers as though trying to read her soul. Slowly, he pulled her closer, his icy embrace sending a shiver down her spine. His breath was a cold gust against her ear, but it was the warmth in his touch that kept her grounded.

"We will face this together, Aeryn," Thorne whispered, his voice rough. "But we have to be prepared. The truth… the truth will tear us apart if we're not careful."

"I'm ready," she said, her voice steady. She didn't know if she truly was, but she had to be. For him. For them.

Thorne pulled back slightly, his icy gaze never leaving hers. "Aeryn, I was born to lead the Iceborn. But I'm also the one who could destroy them. I don't know what that means for us. For our love."

Aeryn placed her hand on his chest, right where his heart beat, the pulse steady beneath her fingers. "It means we fight for each other. It means we break the chains of fate and forge our own path. We don't have to follow the prophecy. We can write our own future."

Thorne's eyes softened at her words, but the fear in them still lingered. His hand reached for hers, his icy fingers brushing against her skin once more. There was a flicker of doubt in his eyes, but there was also something else—a glimmer of hope, small but undeniable.

"I'm scared, Aeryn," Thorne admitted, his voice barely above a whisper. "I'm afraid that I'll lose you. That the prophecy will tear us apart."

Aeryn's heart tightened. She stepped closer to him, her hand gently cupping his face, her thumb brushing the coolness of his cheek. "You won't lose me," she said softly. "You'll never lose me. We're bound, Thorne. And that's what makes us stronger than anything."

For the first time, Thorne seemed to breathe easier, his shoulders relaxing as he looked down at her, his icy resolve beginning to melt. He lowered his forehead to hers, their breaths mingling in the cold air, their hearts beating in sync.

And in that moment, amidst the ruin of their kingdoms, the prophecy, and the storm that raged outside, they realized that their love was not a curse. It was a force. And they would face it together, no matter the cost.

The future was still uncertain. But one thing was clear.

They had made their choice. And that choice was each other.

Together. Forever.

And no prophecy, no storm, could tear them apart.

Thirteen

The Burning Heart

The moon hung high in the sky, casting its pale light over the fractured land. The remains of the Fireborn palace lay before them, a monument to the destruction they had survived, but Aeryn and Thorne knew that their battle was far from over. The storm had passed, but the air still crackled with tension, thick with the weight of the decisions they had yet to make. The very ground beneath their feet seemed to tremble in anticipation, as though the earth itself was holding its breath, waiting for the moment when they would face their true test.

Aeryn stood on the precipice, staring out into the vast expanse, her heart a cacophony of conflicting emotions. She could feel the heat of her fire rising within her, swirling in her chest like an untamed force, but it wasn't the same fire she had once known. It burned differently now, hotter, more dangerous, as if it were responding to something—

someone—inside her. And then there was Thorne, standing beside her, his icy presence a constant reminder of the coldness that had always separated them. His silence had grown heavier with each passing day, his thoughts distant and unreadable.

They had come so far, survived so much, but Aeryn could feel the distance between them growing. Thorne had changed. She had seen it in his eyes, in the way he looked at her now—like he wasn't sure who she was anymore.

Aeryn closed her eyes, trying to steady herself against the onslaught of emotions that swirled inside her. **Fear**. **Doubt**. **Love**. The prophecy had done this to them, twisting everything they thought they knew about themselves and each other. She had always known that the bond they shared would be both a blessing and a curse, but now, it felt like it was suffocating her.

Her fire, once a source of strength, now felt like a threat. The more she reached for it, the more she feared what it might do.

"Aeryn," Thorne's voice broke through her thoughts, low and strained. His voice was distant, as though he, too, was lost in his own turmoil. "We need to talk."

She turned to face him, her heart tightening at the sight of him. He looked different now—darker, more distant, as though he were carrying a weight he didn't know how to shed. The coldness of his power radiated off of him, an unsettling contrast to the warmth of her fire.

"I know," she replied softly, her voice barely above a whisper. "I've been feeling it too. The distance… the weight of everything."

Thorne's expression was unreadable, his eyes shadowed with something that Aeryn couldn't quite place. "We've come so far," he said, his voice rough with emotion. "But it's not enough, Aeryn. We can't keep running from this. We can't keep pretending that everything is going to be okay when it's not."

Her heart ached at his words, the vulnerability in his voice slicing through her like a knife. "I'm not pretending," she said, stepping closer to him. "But we're at a crossroads, Thorne. I feel it too. The pull of the prophecy, the pull of our powers—it's all becoming too much. But we can't let it tear us apart."

Thorne shook his head, his gaze turning away from her, as if he couldn't bear to look at her. "I can't do this anymore, Aeryn. I can't keep pretending that I'm the man you need me to be. I can't keep pretending that I can control this… this storm inside of me."

Aeryn's chest tightened at his words. She had known he was struggling, but hearing him say it out loud felt like a blow. She reached for him, her hand trembling as she touched his arm. "You're not alone in this," she said, her voice pleading. "We've always been together, Thorne. You've always been the one I could turn to. We can face this. Together."

But even as she spoke the words, she felt the weight of the choice hanging over them. The prophecy wasn't just about them anymore—it was about the future of their worlds. They were caught in a web of destiny that neither of them could escape, and no matter how much they loved each other, the forces at play were far greater than them.

Thorne turned to her then, his eyes dark with emotion. "I love you, Aeryn," he whispered, his voice cracking. "But I'm afraid. I'm afraid that if I let you get too close, if I let you see all of me… I might destroy you. I might destroy everything we've built."

Aeryn's heart clenched at the rawness of his words. She could see the pain in his eyes, the fear that had always been there, buried beneath his cold exterior. He was afraid of losing control. But more than that, he was afraid of what his love for her could do.

"I don't care about the prophecy, Thorne," she said fiercely, her voice strong despite the doubt that lingered in her chest. "I care about you. And I don't care how dangerous it is. I'll stand by you, no matter what."

Thorne closed his eyes for a moment, his breath shallow. He looked as though he wanted to say something more, but the words seemed to die on his lips. The silence between them stretched on, heavy with the weight of everything they had yet to say, everything they had yet to face.

Then, the ground beneath them rumbled, shaking violently, and Aeryn gasped as the air around them thickened, the temperature rising and falling in quick bursts. She could feel the power building, the storm that was coming—not just the one from the heavens, but the one that had always been within them. The fire in her chest surged, uncontrollable, and Thorne's icy presence flared in response, his power clashing with hers.

"Aeryn," Thorne said, his voice tight with urgency. "We need to control it. *Now.*"

Aeryn nodded, her heart racing. They had fought together, had survived the worst of the prophecy's effects, but this was different. This was their love, their bond, becoming both their greatest strength and their greatest weakness. She could feel it—the power that surged between them, the heat of her fire, the cold of his ice—and they were both struggling to contain it.

"Thorne, we can't keep holding back," she said, her voice trembling with the weight of the choice she knew they had to make. "We need to unite our powers completely. We have to—"

But before she could finish, the storm erupted around them, the winds howling, the ground shaking beneath their feet. The sky above darkened as the storm grew stronger, a force unlike anything they had ever felt. The very air crackled with energy, the tension between their powers building to a breaking point.

"I can't do it, Aeryn!" Thorne shouted, his voice filled with anguish. "I can't control it. I can't control *us*."

But Aeryn could feel it, feel the bond between them tightening, pulling them closer. They were more than fire and ice—they were one force, one power, and if they didn't embrace it completely, they would both be consumed by it.

Thorne stepped back, his eyes wide with fear. "Aeryn, please… don't ask me to do this."

But Aeryn's heart was already made up. She knew what they had to do. The prophecy had already set their fates in motion, and if they didn't give in to the storm, they would be torn apart. They had to sacrifice everything—every fear, every doubt—if they were to survive.

"I'll risk everything," she said, her voice fierce and steady, though her body shook with the weight of her words. "I'll risk *us* if it means saving everything else."

Thorne's eyes searched hers, the fear in them mingling with something else—something deeper, something he had always kept buried beneath his icy exterior. His breath caught in his chest, and for a moment, it seemed like he might pull away. But then, as though he could no longer fight it, he stepped closer to her, his eyes never leaving hers.

"I trust you," he whispered.

And with those three words, everything changed.

The power surged between them—fire and ice, light and dark, love and fear. It was all-consuming, a force greater than they had ever known. The air around them crackled with electricity, the ground beneath them trembling as the world seemed to hold its breath.

Aeryn felt her fire flare, and Thorne's ice responded in kind. Their powers collided, merged, and for a moment, it felt like the entire world was exploding in a burst of pure energy. The storm around them grew wilder, fiercer, the winds howling in fury as the very elements fought against them.

But then, something shifted. The world around them seemed to fade, and for the briefest moment, it was just them—their love, their power, their bond. The connection between them burned brighter than ever, a light in the darkness, a beacon of hope and destruction.

And then, it happened.

The explosion of fire and ice was blinding, a force so strong it ripped through the very fabric of the world they knew. The ground shattered beneath their feet, the air turned to fire, and for a moment, Aeryn thought she might burn away entirely, consumed by the force of their combined power.

But just as quickly as it had come, the explosion faded, leaving behind only silence.

Aeryn blinked, her body shaking as she stood, her heart pounding in her chest. She turned to Thorne, her breath catching in her throat as she saw him standing before her, his body bloodied, but his eyes filled with a strange calm.

"We did it," Thorne whispered, his voice hoarse but filled with something else—something that had been missing before. There was peace in his gaze now, a peace that came from embracing the storm.

But Aeryn knew that the storm was far from over. The battle had only just begun. They had chosen each other. But the cost of that choice had yet to be revealed.

They had survived. But would their love be enough to save them?

And what would it cost them in the end?

Aeryn's heart pounded in her chest, the air still thick with the residue of their combined power. The remnants of the storm that had surrounded them were beginning to dissipate, the winds dying down, leaving behind a deafening silence. But the silence between her and Thorne felt like a fragile thread, ready to snap at the slightest tug.

She turned to look at him, her breath catching in her throat. Thorne was standing before her, his form strong but battered. His clothes were torn, his skin marked by burns and cuts, but there was something different in his eyes. Something softer. Something that she hadn't seen in him before. But with that softness came something else, something dark—something she had seen before, but never this close.

The power they had unleashed had been both beautiful and terrifying, and now they were left standing in the aftermath, the consequences of their choices hanging like a storm cloud above them.

Thorne's eyes met hers, and for a long moment, neither of them spoke. There was so much left unsaid, so many emotions tangled in the air between them, but there was one thing that was undeniable: they had done it. They had risked everything. They had given themselves completely to the storm—and survived.

"Thorne," Aeryn whispered, her voice trembling. She

reached out to him, her fingers brushing against the coldness of his skin. The ice that had once been so much a part of him now felt different, less sharp, almost like it had been tempered by the warmth of her fire.

His gaze softened slightly, but there was still a wariness in his eyes, a hesitation that made her heart ache. He was still holding back, still unsure.

"I don't know how to feel about this," Thorne said, his voice barely above a whisper, hoarse from the strain of their combined powers. "I never thought it would be like this—never thought that we could actually… combine our forces like that. We've crossed a line, Aeryn."

Aeryn's chest tightened as she stepped closer to him, her hands trembling with both exhaustion and the desire to bridge the distance between them. "We've crossed a lot of lines," she said softly, her voice thick with emotion. "But this was the only way. You and I—our powers, our hearts—we were never meant to be separate. We're part of something bigger than just fire or ice. Together, we're unstoppable."

Thorne's eyes flickered with something that looked like doubt. He stepped back slightly, the coldness of his power making the air between them feel distant again. "But that's the problem, Aeryn. We've always been two halves of something, but we've never been whole. And I'm afraid—afraid that what we've just done, what we've just unleashed—it might be too much. We're both so much stronger now, but what if it's too much for either of us to control?"

Aeryn felt a chill slip into her heart, the same fear she had seen in his eyes now mirrored in her own. She had known the risks, had felt the pulse of the prophecy, but hearing him say it out loud made it all too real. The bond they shared, the power they had unlocked, could either save them or destroy them.

"I don't care if it's too much, Thorne," she said, her voice steady but laced with the weight of her resolve. "I care that we have each other. And we'll figure this out. We have to."

Thorne looked at her, his gaze piercing, searching for something, but it wasn't the same cold judgment she had seen before. There was something softer in him now, something that he had kept hidden for too long.

"I don't know if I can keep you safe," he whispered. "I don't know if I can be the man you deserve. The power inside me— it's darker than you realize. It pulls at me. It's been pulling me my whole life. And the more I fight it, the more it wants to consume everything I've built."

Aeryn shook her head, her hand reaching for him again, this time pulling him closer. She could feel the chill in him, but she didn't flinch. She couldn't.

"I don't want you to be perfect, Thorne," she said, her voice strong but tender. "I want you to be *real*. And I want to be with you, not despite your darkness, but because of it. We both have shadows inside us. We both have parts of us that scare us. But that's what makes us strong. Together, we are more than the sum of our parts. We are fire and ice, yes. But we are also love. And that's a force stronger than anything we've ever known."

For a long moment, Thorne said nothing. His eyes were dark, unreadable, as though he were battling something inside himself. Aeryn could see the fight in him, the fear, the doubt. He wanted to believe her, wanted to believe in the promise they had made to each other, but the burden of the prophecy—of their fate—was a heavy weight on his shoulders.

"Aeryn," Thorne said finally, his voice low, "What if we can't stop it? What if this—what we've just done—isn't enough?

What if the storm that's coming is more than just a force we can control? What if we've already crossed the point of no return?"

Aeryn's breath caught in her throat. The storm. The one they had always known was coming. The one that had been foretold. It wasn't just the battle they had fought together. It was something worse. Something that had been growing inside them all along, pulling them toward their fate.

"I don't know what's coming, Thorne," she said softly, her voice breaking. "But I know that whatever it is, I will face it with you. We don't have to be afraid of the storm. We are the storm."

She could see the struggle in him—the conflict, the hesitation. But he didn't pull away. He didn't retreat. Instead, he reached for her, his cold hand meeting her fiery warmth, their powers merging, both of them trembling from the intensity of their connection.

For the briefest moment, Aeryn felt it—felt the bond between them flare brighter than ever before. They were more than just fire and ice. They were *one*, a force that defied everything. Their love was no longer a mere connection. It was a power, a force that could either save or destroy everything.

And then, without warning, the ground beneath them trembled again, the earth shaking violently as the storm outside picked up again, stronger than before. Aeryn gasped as the wind picked up, howling around them, pulling at their clothes, tearing at their resolve.

It was here. The storm. The one they had been preparing for. The one they couldn't stop.

Aeryn's heart pounded in her chest as she and Thorne stood together, facing the chaos that had been building for so long.

The winds screamed, the sky darkened, and the world seemed to split in two. The prophecy was no longer a distant promise. It was here, now, and they had to face it. They had no choice.

"We have to make a choice, Thorne," Aeryn said, her voice steady despite the terror building inside her. "We can either fight against this… or we can become it."

Thorne's icy gaze met hers, his expression unreadable, but there was something there now, something that hadn't been there before. Hope. Not just hope for survival. But hope for their love.

He took a deep breath and nodded, his hand tightening around hers. "Together," he said simply. "No matter what."

The storm raged around them, but Aeryn and Thorne stood firm, their hearts beating as one. They had faced the fire. They had faced the ice. And now, together, they would face whatever came next.

The world was tearing apart around them, but for the first time, Aeryn knew that they were ready. Whatever the future held, they would face it. Together.

And as the storm raged on, the two of them—bound by love, by fire, by ice—took the first step into the unknown, ready to sacrifice everything for the chance to survive, to love, and to change the fate that had been set for them.

They were ready. And the storm was about to show them how much they truly were.

Fourteen

The Ice Beneath

The land was silent—eerily so—as the final battle loomed on the horizon. The once-proud kingdom of the Fireborn was now little more than a broken shell of what it had been. The wind howled across the barren landscape, carrying with it the remnants of their previous struggle, the echoes of a world on the brink of collapse. The ruins of the Fireborn palace stood before them, an ominous reminder of the war they had already fought and the one still to come.

Aeryn stood at the edge of the crumbled remains, her eyes scanning the horizon, her heart a violent storm of emotions. She could feel it—the weight of the prophecy pressing down on her shoulders, pulling her in a direction she didn't want to go. She had always known the day would come when she would have to face the truth about her fate, but now, standing on the precipice, she wasn't sure she could face the price it would demand.

Beside her, Thorne's presence was a constant, cold shadow. His icy power had always been a part of him, but now, it felt different. His silence was deafening, his distance palpable. There was a flicker of doubt in his eyes, a hesitation that Aeryn could feel like a growing fracture between them. The storm inside him, the fear of what their love might become, had only intensified in the days leading up to this moment. He had become a stranger to her in some ways, but in others, he was still the man she had fought for, the man who had stood by her side through everything.

But the prophecy was real. They couldn't escape it.

"The final battle approaches," Thorne's voice broke through her thoughts, his tone hollow and strained. His eyes flickered toward her, but there was no warmth in them. Only uncertainty.

Aeryn didn't respond right away. Instead, she turned to face him, her heart hammering in her chest. The fire within her flared, but it wasn't the same as before. It was colder now, like it had been tempered by the weight of the decisions they had made. But it was still there, still ready to burn if she let it.

"I know," she said softly, her voice barely above a whisper. "It's here. The storm. The end."

Thorne's gaze hardened, his icy power flaring in response to her words. "We've always known this day would come, Aeryn. But that doesn't make it any easier to face. The prophecy—our bond—it's destroying everything."

Aeryn's chest tightened. "We can still fight it," she said, her voice more forceful now. "We can still defy it."

But the words felt hollow. She knew, deep down, that defying the prophecy wasn't enough. They had already come too far, crossed too many lines. The only way to stop the destruction, to prevent everything they loved from burning away, was to break the chain of fate itself.

And that would require a sacrifice.

"Aeryn, listen to me," Thorne said, his voice suddenly sharper, more urgent. He stepped closer, his eyes searching hers as if looking for something—something that would give him the strength to keep going. "This isn't just about us anymore. It never was. The prophecy isn't just a warning. It's the very core of our existence. We can't keep fighting it. We can't keep running from what we are."

Aeryn's heart clenched. She knew what he was saying, knew what he meant. The prophecy had always been the force that controlled them, shaping their fates, pulling them toward a future they couldn't avoid. But now, in the silence of the ruins, she could feel it—the truth of their situation. The only way to change the course of the prophecy, to prevent the destruction that loomed over both kingdoms, was to break the chain that had bound them all along.

"Thorne," she whispered, stepping closer, her voice thick with emotion. "We can break it. We can *choose* our own path. We don't have to let the prophecy control us."

Thorne's icy eyes narrowed. "You don't understand," he said, his voice shaking. "It's not that simple. You don't know what it would cost."

Aeryn's breath caught in her throat. The truth of it—the gravity of the decision they had to make—was becoming clearer with every passing moment. The prophecy had always promised destruction. The love between fire and ice was not meant to be a union of peace. It was meant to tear both kingdoms apart.

But they weren't just fire and ice. They were *more* than that. They were love, and that love could be their salvation—or their undoing.

"Aeryn," Thorne said again, his voice rough. "I can feel it—feel the storm inside me. The longer I fight it, the more it pulls at me. It's *you* and *me*, Aeryn. The prophecy is our bond. Our love. And no matter how much we fight it, we are the ones who will bring about the end of everything. It's always been us."

Aeryn shook her head, her pulse quickening as the weight of his words crushed down on her. "No, Thorne. It's not about the prophecy anymore. It's about *us*. What we've built. What we *can* build. The only way to stop it is to break the chain of fate. To make a choice that isn't dictated by what the prophecy says."

Thorne looked at her, his expression unreadable, the coldness of his power now swirling around them both. But she could see it—see the fear in his eyes, the doubt that had always been there, lurking beneath the surface. It was the same fear that had kept him distant, the fear that their love could destroy everything.

But Aeryn wasn't afraid anymore.

She stepped forward, her hand trembling as she reached for him. "Thorne, we can't let this define us. We *define* it. We've already proven that we can fight it. We've survived everything they've thrown at us. We can survive this too."

His gaze flickered, but the ice that surrounded him remained. "I don't know if I can do it. I don't know if I can be the man you need me to be."

The words hit her like a blow, but Aeryn didn't flinch. She reached out, her hand covering his, feeling the coldness that radiated from him. "You don't need to be perfect, Thorne. You need to be *real*. I've never wanted you to be anything else."

For a moment, Thorne's eyes softened, the coldness flickering, and Aeryn felt the warmth of their bond begin to reignite. But it was fleeting. The tension still hung heavy between them.

The storm outside intensified again, but this time, it wasn't just the wind that howled. The earth beneath their feet trembled as if the very ground was shaking at the impending conflict. The storm was coming, and it was bigger than either of them could imagine.

Thorne took a deep breath, his icy fingers tightening around hers. "Aeryn," he said, his voice barely above a whisper. "If we break the chain of fate, if we truly defy the prophecy… what will it cost us? What will we lose?"

Aeryn's chest tightened as the truth settled in. "We may lose everything, Thorne. But we have to choose. If we don't, the world will be lost anyway. The prophecy isn't just about us— it's about our worlds. We either fight for them… or we let them burn."

Thorne's expression hardened, his jaw clenching as he looked out over the ruins of the kingdom. The weight of the decision, the gravity of what they had to face, seemed to crush him. But he didn't pull away. He didn't turn from her.

"What if the cost is us?" he asked, his voice a raw whisper.

Aeryn's heart cracked. She knew what he was asking. The ultimate price. But she had already made her choice.

She stepped closer to him, her hand resting against his chest, feeling the beat of his heart beneath her fingers. "Then I will pay it," she said softly. "I will pay it for us. For them. For the future."

The world around them seemed to freeze as their powers

collided again—fire and ice, swirling and merging, pushing against each other with a force that could destroy everything they had ever known. The storm was inside them now, and Aeryn felt the heat of her fire struggling to contain the cold that surged from Thorne.

"We can't hold back anymore," she said, her voice barely audible over the roar of their combined powers. "We have to face it."

Thorne's icy eyes locked onto hers, and for a moment, time seemed to stop. The world around them was silent. And then, slowly, he nodded. "Together," he whispered, his voice thick with emotion.

Together.

Aeryn felt the fire in her chest surge, and Thorne's ice followed, wrapping around her like a shield. They had no choice now. They had to make this choice. To risk everything. To break the chains that had bound them.

With one final surge, the power within them flared, a force that sent shockwaves through the very earth, tearing apart the ruins around them. The ground shook violently as the storm outside grew even fiercer, but within them, within their hearts, there was nothing but the choice to fight.

And as the storm raged, Aeryn knew one thing for certain: the prophecy had never been about their destruction. It had always been about their *choice*—their choice to fight for each other, for the future, for love.

But there was still one thing they had yet to face.

The cost of that choice.

And whether they could survive the storm that would follow.

Aeryn felt the surge of power between them as it reached its peak—a violent clash of fire and ice, a force so immense it threatened to tear apart everything they had ever known. The ground beneath them trembled, the very earth shuddering as if the world itself was reacting to the chaos they had unleashed. Her heart raced, the heat of her flames struggling to contain the cold that radiated from Thorne. The storm they had summoned was not just the fury of their powers; it was the storm of their very hearts—the storm that would either destroy them or set them free.

Thorne's icy presence pressed against her, a constant, overwhelming chill, but it no longer felt like a barrier. No, this time, their powers—fire and ice—had merged, become something more. They were no longer two separate forces warring against each other. They were *one*, a force so powerful that it felt like the very fabric of reality was bending beneath them.

Aeryn's breath caught in her throat as the energy between them crackled, a sharp electric tension in the air, so thick it felt as though she could reach out and touch it. They were standing on the edge of something monumental—a precipice that could either bring salvation or doom.

"Thorne," she breathed, her voice strained as the storm intensified, the winds howling, the sky above them growing darker, swirling with the fury of their combined powers. The temperature was rising and falling in chaotic waves, the heat of her fire clashing against the bitter cold of his ice. They were locked in a battle, not just of elements, but of their very souls, their hearts fighting to find balance in the chaos.

But in the midst of this violent whirlwind, Aeryn saw something in Thorne's eyes—something that flickered beneath the cold, beneath the fear. It was a spark of resolve, of understanding. They had made their choice. The prophecy, the storm, the destruction—they could not be allowed to define them any longer. They were more than that. Together, they were the only force capable of shaping their own future.

But the sacrifice was still there, looming, like a dark cloud that hovered above them both. It was a cost neither of them had fully realized until now.

Thorne's grip on her tightened, his cold fingers pressing into her skin, but instead of pulling away, he pulled her closer, drawing her into the epicenter of their combined power. The ground beneath them cracked open, a deep, violent fissure splitting through the ruins as the force of their love and their power combined.

"I can feel it, Aeryn," Thorne whispered, his voice shaky, the ice in his tone now replaced by something raw, something uncertain. "The power is too much. It's burning inside me, and I don't know how to stop it."

Aeryn looked up at him, her heart heavy with the understanding of what he was saying. The love they had was a force unlike anything they had ever known. It was *their* power— more than just fire and ice, more than the prophecy. But it was also their greatest danger. The more they tried to hold it back, the more it threatened to consume them both.

"No," Aeryn said, her voice firm despite the fear that threatened to overtake her. She reached up to touch his face, the warmth of her fire brushing against the cold of his ice. "We control it. We *choose* it. The prophecy never said we had to destroy each other. It only said that one of us would be the end of everything." She paused, her breath catching in her throat. "But it never said we couldn't rewrite it."

Thorne's eyes locked onto hers, the cold flicker of doubt still lingering, but there was something else there now—a flicker of hope. He had always feared what they were becoming, what they could do together. But in this moment, he saw it too. They weren't bound by fate. They were bound by something stronger: *love.* And that love was more powerful than any prophecy, any curse.

His icy power flared one last time, wrapping around her like a shield, but Aeryn didn't step back. She felt the fire inside her, the power, burning brighter and hotter. They were *together.* No more fear. No more doubts. They were two halves of a whole—two forces meant to change the world, not destroy it.

"Together," she whispered, her voice barely audible over the roar of their combined powers. "We fight together."

Thorne closed his eyes for a moment, his expression tightening, as though the weight of their decision was finally settling in. He was afraid. She could feel it in the way his body trembled beneath her touch. But he wasn't backing down. Not anymore.

"Yes," he said softly, his voice thick with emotion. "Together."

And with those words, the final act began. The air around them surged, their powers colliding in an explosion that lit up the darkened sky. The force of it was unlike anything they had ever felt before. The earth cracked beneath their feet, the storm around them rising to an impossible intensity, but Aeryn and Thorne stood firm, their love now a force so powerful it threatened to tear the world apart.

The ground beneath them shattered, sending them both to their knees, but they didn't fall apart. Their powers swirled around them, fire and ice blending in a whirlwind that pulsed with the very essence of their bond.

"Aeryn…" Thorne's voice was broken, his chest heaving as he fought to keep his control. "We can't stop it. We can't control what we've become."

But Aeryn shook her head, her heart burning with the fire of conviction. "We *are* in control, Thorne. We decide this. We choose to rewrite the prophecy. We choose to live."

She pressed her hand against his chest, feeling the powerful beating of his heart beneath her fingers. His icy exterior had melted, leaving only the man she loved, the man who had stood beside her through everything. She could feel his heart, his soul, intertwining with hers. They were no longer separate. They were *one*.

The storm raged around them, but Aeryn and Thorne stood together in the center of it, their love a beacon that pushed back against the darkness.

Then, in that final moment, when it felt like the world itself was about to explode, Aeryn realized what she had to do. The choice had always been hers—had always been theirs. They could not allow the prophecy to bind them any longer. They had to break free.

But breaking free would come at a price.

The bond between them flared, and Aeryn felt the heat of her fire surge one last time. Thorne's ice, too, rose in a violent crescendo. She could feel it—the power that could either save them or destroy them.

In that final moment, she understood what the sacrifice would be. To break the prophecy—to choose their own future—they would both have to give something. The cost would be *everything*.

Aeryn's heart shattered as she whispered the final words. "Thorne, we have to let go. We have to let the fire and the ice merge completely. To do that, we'll have to give up everything. All the fear, all the doubt, all the power. We have to give ourselves up to it."

Thorne's eyes widened in horror, but there was something else in them—something understanding. He understood now. He saw it for what it was.

They had to burn away the prophecy. They had to destroy it from the inside.

"No!" Thorne cried out, reaching for her, his icy fingers trembling as he grasped her hand. "I can't lose you, Aeryn. I can't—"

But Aeryn's gaze was steady, her hand squeezing his. "We will always be together. Even if we have to let go of everything."

And then, as their powers surged one final time, they let go. They allowed the fire and ice to consume them completely, their souls intertwining in an explosion of light and darkness, a force so pure that it ripped through the very fabric of reality itself.

And in that moment, the prophecy was no more.

They had rewritten their fate.

But the cost—oh, the cost—was something neither of them had fully understood until the very end.

Fifteen

The Frozen Kiss

The air was thick with the weight of impending destruction. The storm had returned—darker, fiercer than before. The sky churned with the fury of the elements, and Aeryn could feel the electricity in the air, the crackling charge that hummed beneath her skin. It was the calm before the storm, but she knew, deep down, that the storm had already begun. The battle they had fought, the sacrifices they had made, had led them to this moment. And no matter how much they had hoped for another way, there was no turning back.

Thorne stood beside her, his ice-cold presence a constant reminder of everything they had faced, everything they had become. His eyes, once sharp with fear and uncertainty, now burned with something else—something she had seen before, but never like this. It was a quiet, devastating resolve. A resolve that matched her own.

The weight of the prophecy, the chains of fate that had bound them together, had been leading them here for so long. They had fought against it, yes. But in the end, the prophecy would not be denied. And they both knew it. One of them had to fall. The balance between fire and ice had to be struck, and the cost would be their love.

Aeryn's breath hitched as she turned toward Thorne, her heart pounding in her chest. The world around them seemed to blur, the noise of the storm deafening in her ears. But all she could hear was the rush of blood in her veins and the steady rhythm of his heart, so close to hers.

Thorne's face was unreadable, but the tension in his body was palpable. She could feel it in the way his shoulders were tight, in the way his breath came in shallow gasps. The cold that radiated from him was more than just a physical force; it was the reflection of the fear he was holding inside. The fear of losing her. The fear of what he might have to do to save her.

"Thorne," Aeryn whispered, stepping closer to him. Her voice trembled, but her heart was steady. She could feel it—she could feel the pull of their bond, the fire inside her rising in response to his presence. It was a force unlike anything they had ever experienced, and now, it was pulling them together. One last time.

His icy gaze met hers, his expression torn. "Aeryn… we can't stop this. We can't stop what's coming."

Aeryn reached for him, her fingers trembling as she touched his cold cheek. The heat of her fire was nothing compared to the chill that surrounded him. She could feel it—the tension between them, the fierce love they shared, and the knowledge that it was all about to end.

"I know," she whispered, her voice breaking. "But I *won't* let it end like this, Thorne. Not without a fight. Not without us."

He closed his eyes for a moment, as though the weight of her words was enough to break the dam inside him. When he opened them again, they were filled with something—something softer, something that spoke of a love so deep, so raw, that it could burn brighter than any fire.

"Aeryn," Thorne said, his voice a low rasp. He took a step closer, closing the distance between them until they were standing chest to chest. His hand reached for hers, and when their fingers touched, a jolt of heat and ice surged through her, a reminder of everything they were. Everything they had become.

The storm outside raged louder, the winds howling with the fury of the world around them, but inside this moment, inside the space they shared, it was just them. The fire and ice. The love that had both destroyed and saved them. And now, in the face of the inevitable, they were bound by that love. They had no choice but to face it.

"Aeryn," Thorne said again, his voice barely audible over the roar of the storm. "I love you."

The words hit her like a tidal wave, crashing over her, drowning her in the intensity of his emotion. She had heard those words before, but never like this. Never with the weight of everything they had been through, everything they had fought for, hanging between them.

"I love you too, Thorne," Aeryn whispered, her heart breaking. "Always."

He leaned in, his breath cold against her skin, and for a brief moment, the world seemed to stop. All of the pain, the fear, the loss—it melted away. There was only the two of them, standing together in the midst of the chaos they had created.

There was only the love they shared, the love that had been their salvation.

And then, without a word, Thorne kissed her.

It was a kiss unlike any they had shared before. It was desperate, raw, a last-ditch effort to hold on to what they had. The cold of his lips against hers was like nothing she had ever felt—sharp, biting, but also comforting, as if the chill of his power was all she had ever known. Her fire responded in kind, flaring inside her, warming the cold spaces between them. Their powers surged together, fire and ice clashing and merging in a violent, beautiful symphony that sent shockwaves through the air around them.

But in that moment, Aeryn realized something.

This was it.

This was the end.

Their love, their bond, had always been a source of power— and now, it was the one thing that would either save them or destroy them. The prophecy had always said that one would die, but what it hadn't said was that the one who fell might be the one who saved the other. It hadn't said that the power of their love could transcend fate itself. It hadn't said that they could rewrite their future, even at the cost of their own lives.

And Aeryn knew, with a heart-wrenching clarity, that to break the chain of fate, to stop the destruction, one of them would have to fall. And that fall—no matter who it was—would be the sacrifice that would save the world.

But she couldn't bring herself to say the words. She couldn't bring herself to make the choice between them.

The kiss deepened, the force of their powers growing stronger, but Aeryn could feel it. She could feel the heat of the fire and the chill of the ice surging through her, pulling them both toward the breaking point. They were reaching the apex, the moment when everything would either come crashing down—or change forever.

Thorne's body shuddered beneath her touch, his coldness growing, his powers battling against her fire. It was more than just a physical battle—it was a battle of wills, of destinies. And in that moment, Aeryn realized what they had to do.

With a sharp gasp, she broke the kiss, pulling back just enough to look into his eyes. There was fear there, yes, but there was also love. So much love. The kind of love that could change the world. The kind of love that could save them, even if it meant destroying themselves in the process.

"Thorne," she whispered, her voice shaking with the intensity of what she was about to say. "We have to choose. This is the only way. The only way to save them all."

Thorne's breath was ragged, his chest rising and falling with the weight of what they both knew. But his eyes never left hers. "Aeryn…" he said, his voice trembling, the coldness of his power faltering as he let the warmth of her fire seep into him. "I can't lose you. I can't… be without you."

The pain in his voice shattered something inside her, but she pressed her forehead to his, her hand trembling as it cupped his face. "You won't lose me, Thorne. I'll always be with you. We'll always be together."

And with those words, the storm inside them reached its peak.

The world around them shook, the ground splitting beneath them, as if the earth itself was about to crumble under the weight of their powers. The wind howled, the sky lit up with streaks of lightning, and the air around them shimmered with the heat of their fire and the cold of his ice. It was as though the universe was holding its breath, waiting for them to make the ultimate choice.

And then, without a single word, Aeryn felt it—felt the shift as they both let go. They allowed their powers to merge completely, fire and ice blending into one unstoppable force, a blinding explosion of light and darkness that tore through the very fabric of the world they knew.

Aeryn's body shook as she felt herself being pulled into the storm, her heart racing as the fire and ice consumed her. Thorne was with her, his presence still a constant, but the pull of their combined powers was overwhelming. She could feel him slipping away, feel the cost of the sacrifice they were both making.

In that final moment, when the storm reached its peak and the world seemed to shatter around them, Aeryn realized the truth. Their love had transcended fate itself. They had rewritten the prophecy. And whatever happened next, whatever the cost, their love had been worth it.

For in that moment of destruction, they were reborn.

And the world, no matter how much it tore at them, would never be the same again.

The blinding force of their combined powers surged through the very fabric of the world. Fire and ice, once opposing elements, now fused into one unstoppable storm of energy. The ground beneath them cracked and splintered, the air thick with a crackling charge as the earth itself seemed to shudder at the intensity of the force they had unleashed. Aeryn's pulse raced, her heart pounding in her chest as she felt the weight of their actions—of their sacrifice—pressing down on her like a heavy stone.

Thorne's presence beside her was a constant, his icy power entwined with hers, but there was something in the way the world was trembling that felt wrong. The air was thick with the scent of burning ozone and cold steel, and she could feel the finality of the moment as it pressed down on them. The prophecy, the storm, the love they had fought for—it was all coming to a head now.

Aeryn's breath caught in her throat as she felt her body start to crumble under the intensity of their merged powers. The fire within her, the energy she had always controlled, was now wild, uncontrollable, and it clashed violently with Thorne's ice. The cold within him had always been a constant, a shield, but now it felt as though it were slowly consuming them both. The balance they had fought so hard to maintain was beginning to unravel, and there was no way to stop it.

"Thorne," Aeryn gasped, her voice breaking through the whirlwind of power around them. "Thorne, we have to—"

But the words died in her throat as the world around them fractured further, the very air splitting apart as the forces they had unleashed tore through the sky. She reached for him, her hand trembling as it slid across his cold skin, the ice of his power pressing against her fiery warmth, and for a moment, everything went still.

Thorne's icy eyes met hers, and she saw it then—the same thing she had feared in his gaze all along. The same fear that had been building within him, the same reluctance he had tried so desperately to push aside. It was a look of understanding. Of acceptance. But also of goodbye.

"Aeryn," Thorne's voice was hoarse, strained, the coldness that surrounded him now a reflection of the despair within. "You've always been the fire, the warmth, the light. I... I can't keep you safe anymore. This is how it ends. One of us has to fall."

Tears welled in Aeryn's eyes as she reached for him, her fingers brushing against his cheek, feeling the cold that had always been so familiar to her but now felt like a sharp contrast to the heat inside her. She couldn't speak, couldn't find the words to make him understand. Because deep down, she knew it too. She knew that the prophecy wasn't just about the balance of fire and ice. It was about the cost of their love, the price they had to pay for defying fate.

"No, Thorne," she whispered fiercely, her voice breaking. "I won't let you die. Not like this. Not because of me."

His eyes softened, but the pain in them was unbearable. "Aeryn…"

She didn't let him finish. She couldn't. Instead, she pulled him toward her, her arms wrapping around him, pulling him into a kiss that was both a plea and a declaration. Their lips met in a desperate, soul-shattering kiss—raw, urgent, and filled with everything they had never said. The fire inside her flared with a force that felt like it would consume them both, and she could feel the ice in Thorne's body shudder against the intensity of her power. For a brief moment, it felt like they were suspended in time—fire and ice, love and sacrifice—holding onto each other as the world around them crumbled.

But that moment didn't last. The world began to crack once more, the storm around them growing even fiercer. The energy between them pulsed, a raw, chaotic force that pushed them apart even as they clung to each other. The ground beneath them splintered further, and Aeryn felt the storm— both inside her and around her—growing more violent. The destruction was inevitable.

"Thorne!" Aeryn cried out, her voice breaking as she stepped back, her hand still holding onto his, but the space between them was widening. She could feel it—the inevitable pull of the prophecy, the fact that one of them had to die. And the price for their love was the life of one of them.

Thorne's eyes locked onto hers, his expression a mixture of resignation and love. "Aeryn…" He stopped, his voice catching in his throat, and Aeryn felt her heart shatter. "I love you."

The words were a whisper, a final confession, and they cut through Aeryn's soul. But it wasn't enough. It could never be enough.

Before she could respond, Thorne's icy power flared one final time, and the blast knocked her backward. The force of it sent her sprawling to the ground, and the world around her exploded into light.

The storm raged above, the winds howling, the earth shaking, but in that moment, nothing mattered except Thorne. Her body was shaking, her heart aching with the knowledge that she couldn't stop what was happening. She could feel the weight of the prophecy crushing down on them both.

Thorne had made his choice.

Aeryn struggled to her feet, but it was too late. The world around her seemed to collapse into nothingness, the storm growing louder, more violent. Thorne was standing in the center of the devastation, his ice-blue eyes filled with an emotion Aeryn couldn't quite place. There was love, yes, but there was something else—something darker.

The storm inside him had reached its peak.

"Aeryn," Thorne said, his voice cold but filled with an undeniable sense of finality. "This is the only way. You have to let me go."

Aeryn reached out for him, her heart breaking in her chest, but the air around them seemed to twist, to distort, as though the very fabric of reality was unraveling. The temperature plummeted, and Aeryn could feel her fire flickering, struggling against the overwhelming cold that consumed Thorne.

"I won't let you go, Thorne," she cried out, her voice ragged. "I can't—"

But his gaze never wavered. He was already slipping away, his body trembling as the icy energy within him grew stronger. The storm roared around them, and Aeryn could feel it—the final clash between fire and ice, the ultimate sacrifice that would either save them or destroy everything they had fought for.

Thorne's lips parted as if to speak, but then the storm flared once more, the violent burst of energy surging through the air. Aeryn felt it—the end was coming. She reached for him, but the force of the storm was too great. The explosion of ice and fire consumed them both.

Time seemed to slow. Aeryn's chest tightened as the storm raged around them, and she watched as Thorne—her Thorne— disappeared into the chaos. The cold of his ice, the warmth of her fire—both were lost in the storm, swallowed by the forces they had unleashed.

And then, the world went still.

Aeryn gasped, her chest heaving as she fell to her knees, her mind a blur. The storm had passed. The world had stopped shaking. But it felt wrong. It felt empty. She reached out for him, her hand trembling as it searched for any sign of him, but there was nothing. Only the silence.

The cost had been too great.

Tears filled her eyes, and she allowed them to fall, the weight of the loss crashing down on her like a wave. Thorne had sacrificed everything for them—everything they had fought for, everything they had been.

And now, she was left with nothing.

But in the deepest corner of her heart, a flicker of hope remained. Their love had transcended fate. Their bond had shattered the prophecy. Even in death, they had rewritten their story. They had defied everything that had tried to tear them apart.

And that, Aeryn realized, was their greatest victory.

Thorne was gone, but his love—his sacrifice—would live on forever.

And for the first time, as the storm finally began to calm, Aeryn understood the true cost of their love. It wasn't just about fire and ice. It was about what they had created together.

And that, she knew, would never die.

Sixteen

The Last Sacrifice

The ground beneath Aeryn's feet trembled, the air around her humming with the chaos of the final battle. The storm raged overhead, a twisted fusion of fire and ice, a reflection of the love and destruction that had defined her existence. Her heart hammered in her chest, the weight of the prophecy hanging over her like an iron shackle. They had fought. They had defied fate. But now, the price of their defiance had come. It was a choice that would determine the fate of everything they had fought for.

Thorne stood before her, his once ice-blue eyes now clouded with pain, the cold of his power twisting in unnatural ways. His body trembled with the strain of holding back the storm inside him, but Aeryn could feel the danger in the air. She knew it— she could feel the surge of his energy, the threat of his power becoming something uncontrollable. They had come so far, but now the moment of reckoning had arrived.

"Thorne," Aeryn breathed, her voice shaky. The winds howled, pulling at her clothes and hair, but she couldn't look away from him. She couldn't stop herself from reaching out, her hand trembling as she touched his arm, feeling the coldness that radiated from him, but also the warmth of their shared bond. "You have to stop this. It's too much. You're not just hurting yourself anymore. You're hurting everyone."

Thorne's gaze flickered toward her, his lips parted as if to speak, but his voice was swallowed by the roar of the battle. His ice-cold power pulsed around them both, swirling like a storm that could destroy everything in its path. The earth trembled again, and Aeryn could feel the pull of their love—the pull of their power—growing stronger by the second.

"I can't control it anymore," Thorne said, his voice rough, the weight of despair in his words. He took a step back, his body shaking with the strain of keeping the storm at bay. "The prophecy… it was never just about us, Aeryn. It was about our worlds. The balance has been destroyed. I'm the one who will bring the end."

"No." Aeryn's heart clenched, and she stepped forward, her hands reaching for him, desperate. "You're not the end, Thorne. You're my *beginning*. Together, we can stop this. We can still fix everything."

But even as she said the words, she could feel it—the breaking point. The last tether of hope that had bound them together was snapping, unraveling before her eyes. The storm raged around them, and Aeryn felt the heat of her fire clash with the freezing cold of Thorne's power. The battle was raging outside, but within this moment, between them, there was something even more dangerous. The truth. The sacrifice that had been looming since the beginning.

"I'm not the answer," Thorne said, his voice breaking as his eyes met hers. "I've always been the weapon, Aeryn. The prophecy wasn't about us being together. It was about *this*. Our love, our powers, they were never meant to be combined. They were meant to destroy."

Aeryn's chest tightened as she shook her head, refusing to believe it. She stepped closer to him, the fire inside her sparking, but not with anger—no, this was the fire of love, the fire that had always driven her to fight for him, for them.

"No, Thorne. The prophecy doesn't control us anymore. You *and I* decide what happens next. We decide our future."

Thorne's eyes filled with a mixture of anguish and desperation. "But what if I can't control it? What if we can't?"

Aeryn's breath hitched as she reached for him, her hands trembling as they found his icy, cold skin. The storm raged around them, their love—a blazing inferno—colliding with his cold, biting power. For a moment, it felt like the entire world was swirling around them, like they were the center of a maelstrom that would tear them apart. But she wouldn't let go. She couldn't.

"I won't let you go, Thorne," Aeryn said softly, her voice breaking as she placed her hand over his chest, feeling the unsteady rhythm of his heartbeat beneath her fingertips. "I will never let you go."

The words hung between them, heavy with meaning, filled with everything they had fought for and everything they had to lose. But as Aeryn gazed into his eyes, she realized the truth—no matter how much they loved each other, no matter how strong their bond was, it wasn't enough to fight fate alone. The prophecy had always been more than just words—it was the force that had shaped them both, that had guided them to this final choice.

And now it was time to make it.

"You have to choose, Aeryn," Thorne whispered, his voice raw, pleading. "You have to choose between *us* and *everything else*. If you try to save me, if you try to stop this, it will destroy both kingdoms. You know what I have to do. You know what must happen."

Aeryn's heart shattered at the weight of his words, the truth of the sacrifice hanging between them like a blade. Her hand, still resting over his chest, felt the steady beat of his heart. The steady beat that, for so long, had been the rhythm of her own. And now, she could feel it slipping away. She could feel the storm—the cold and the fire—raging, overwhelming them both.

"You want me to let you go," Aeryn whispered, her voice thick with emotion. "But I can't, Thorne. I can't live in a world without you."

Thorne closed his eyes, his head lowering as the weight of their situation pressed down on him. "Then *this* will be the end. Our love, Aeryn—it was always meant to be the end."

Aeryn felt the tears she had been holding back finally spill over, her fingers trembling against his chest. She had fought so hard to believe that love could defy fate. She had fought to believe in the future they could have together. But now, the truth of it was undeniable. The prophecy had never been about their love. It had been about their destruction.

"No," she said, her voice fierce, despite the rawness of her emotions. "We decide. Not the prophecy. Not fate."

A sound—a low, rumbling crack—sounded beneath them. The ground trembled again, and the walls of the ruined palace began to collapse around them. The battle outside was nearing its peak, the forces of fire and ice clashing, the future of both kingdoms hanging in the balance. But inside the storm that had consumed Aeryn and Thorne, there was only the unbearable weight of the decision that would change everything.

In that moment, Aeryn knew what she had to do.

"I love you," she whispered, her voice hoarse as she stepped back, her hand slipping from his chest. "But I won't let you destroy everything we've fought for."

Thorne's eyes widened in shock as he stepped forward, reaching for her. "Aeryn, no. Don't—"

But it was too late.

With a final, desperate breath, Aeryn stepped away, feeling the energy surge inside her, the fire within her growing brighter, hotter, wilder. She could feel the power of their love coursing through her veins, but she also felt the ice within Thorne—a coldness that was consuming him.

With a cry, Aeryn thrust her hands forward, pushing the fire inside her out toward him, not to destroy him, but to *free him*. The flames roared as they surged toward Thorne, but this time, it wasn't an attack. It was a plea for release. For peace.

Thorne's body arched in pain, his ice fighting against her flames, but it was no longer a battle of power. It was a battle of their souls, of their bond.

"Aeryn…" Thorne's voice was barely a whisper, his hands reaching for her as the flames surrounded him, consuming the ice inside him.

The air crackled with energy, and Aeryn could feel herself weakening, her body trembling under the strain of their combined powers. The force of her love, her sacrifice, was overwhelming, but she pushed forward, her eyes never leaving his.

"I'm sorry," she whispered, as the fire and ice collided in a brilliant explosion of light and sound.

The world seemed to break apart around them, the storm reaching its apex, the very fabric of reality tearing as their powers merged. And then, in that final moment, everything went still.

Aeryn's body crumpled to the ground, her vision fading as the last remnants of her strength slipped away. The storm outside had calmed. The earth was still.

But as the darkness closed in, one thing was clear.

She had made her choice.

And as the world fell silent, Aeryn knew that even if they were lost, their love would transcend fate itself.

Aeryn's body lay still on the cold, cracked earth, her chest heaving with the weight of the sacrifice she had just made. The air around her, once crackling with energy, had gone eerily still. The storm that had raged in the heavens above them, a furious battle of fire and ice, had finally fallen silent, leaving only the quiet hum of the earth beneath her.

Her vision blurred as the world around her seemed to slip away, the edges of reality fading into a shadow. She could still feel the heat of the fire that had surged within her—the power she had summoned to save them both. And in her mind's eye, she saw Thorne, his form blurred by the storm, reaching out for her, his face a mixture of agony and desperation.

"Aeryn..."

His voice echoed in her ears, a soft, tortured whisper that filled the silence. It was the last thing she heard before the world completely darkened.

But even in the darkness, there was something—something

familiar, something warm. She could feel it, a pull, a presence that reached out to her across the void. Slowly, her eyelids fluttered open, and the world around her came into focus.

Thorne.

He was standing before her, his face pale, but his eyes—his eyes were *alive*. Alive in a way she hadn't seen before. His icy power, once a constant, no longer radiated cold. The storm that had consumed him was gone, replaced by something different, something brighter. It was as though the fire within her, the love they had shared, had somehow reshaped him.

"Aeryn," he whispered again, his voice hoarse but filled with wonder. "You—you're still here."

The words seemed to break something inside her, and Aeryn's breath caught in her throat. She tried to sit up, but the weight of what had just transpired—the power, the storm, the sacrifice—was still too much. Her body ached, her heart heavy with the knowledge of the choice she had made.

"Thorne…" Her voice was weak, barely audible, but it was enough. Enough for him to hear her, enough for him to see the truth in her eyes.

He knelt beside her, his cold fingers touching her face, but it wasn't the biting cold she had known before. It was different now—softer, almost tender. The warmth of their bond had somehow melted the ice that had always kept them apart. And in that warmth, Aeryn felt the truth of it. The truth of their love.

The prophecy had been broken.

"Is it over?" Aeryn asked, her voice shaking, her body trembling as the realization of what they had done settled over her like a shroud. "Did we… did we succeed?"

Thorne nodded slowly, his expression unreadable, yet there

was a flicker of something in his eyes—something between hope and sorrow. "The battle is over. The storm has passed. The prophecy... it's been rewritten."

Aeryn's heart clenched in her chest. It was done. The cost had been paid, the world had been saved, but at what price? The realization of the sacrifice she had made—the final choice that had taken them to the brink—was enough to break her spirit. She had chosen love over fate. She had chosen *him*.

But was it enough?

She reached out for him, her hand trembling as she touched his arm. His eyes met hers, and in that moment, Aeryn could see it—see the reflection of her own emotions in his gaze. There was love, yes, but there was something else too. A deep, profound sorrow. The kind of sorrow that only comes with the knowledge of what was lost.

"I should have been the one to go," Thorne whispered, his voice thick with guilt. "You shouldn't have had to make that choice."

Aeryn shook her head weakly, her fingers still gripping his arm. "No, Thorne. You... you gave everything for me. For us. I couldn't have done this without you."

Thorne's eyes darkened with an emotion Aeryn couldn't quite place. "I almost lost you," he said, his voice breaking. "I thought... I thought I was too late. The power we unleashed—it almost consumed you."

"I'm here," she said softly, her voice gentle despite the tremor of exhaustion that ran through her body. "We're both here. And that's all that matters."

A long silence passed between them, the world around them slowly coming to life as the storm cleared, leaving behind only the remnants of the devastation they had caused. The land, once scarred by the battles of fire and ice, now felt still, peaceful in the aftermath of everything they had fought for.

But the silence between them was filled with the weight of the knowledge that their love, their choice, had saved everything. The world would rebuild. The kingdoms would heal. And though their love had been the catalyst for the destruction and the salvation, it had also become their redemption.

Aeryn's heart pounded in her chest as she looked up at Thorne, her hand reaching for his once more. This time, he didn't pull away. He met her halfway, his fingers intertwining with hers in a gesture that spoke more than words ever could.

"We've lost so much," Thorne whispered, his voice rough, but there was a soft warmth there now. "But we have each other."

Aeryn's chest tightened, the weight of everything they had been through and everything they had lost settling heavily on her heart. "We've lost more than just the battle. We've lost a future that was never meant to be. We've lost a part of ourselves."

Thorne nodded, his eyes dimmed with the sorrow of everything that had been taken from them. But there was something else there—something that Aeryn couldn't quite explain. It was as if, in the aftermath of everything, they had both come to understand that love, even in its most painful and destructive forms, had changed them. It had shaped them into something greater than they ever could have been alone.

"I will always love you, Aeryn," Thorne said, his voice barely a whisper, but it was enough. It was everything. "No matter what happens. No matter what we've lost. You are everything to me."

The words hit Aeryn like a wave, drowning her in the truth

of them. She had never doubted their love, but hearing him say it, feeling the weight of it in his voice, broke something inside her. She had fought so hard for this moment, for this love, and now, in the silence of their victory, she could feel the magnitude of what they had won—and what they had lost.

"I love you, Thorne," Aeryn said softly, her voice breaking. "Always."

And in that final, heart-wrenching moment, as the storm faded into memory, the fire within her and the ice within him merged together once more—not as opposing forces, but as one. Together, they had rewritten their fate, broken the chains of the prophecy, and defied the destruction that had been foretold.

But as the world began to heal, they both knew that the true cost of their love was still yet to be realized. The sacrifice had been made. The world had been saved. And now, as the silence stretched between them, they were left to rebuild not just the kingdoms, but their lives. Their love had survived. But the question that lingered in the air, unanswered, was whether that love could survive the weight of everything they had sacrificed.

For in the end, there was no true victory without loss. But Aeryn knew, with every part of her being, that their love had been worth it.

And together, they would face whatever came next. No matter the cost.

Seventeen

The Shattered Kingdoms

The sun hung low in the sky, casting a pale, blood-red glow over the ruins of what had once been a world of fire and ice. The wind howled through the remains of the crumbled kingdom, carrying with it the stench of smoke and the weight of countless lost lives. Aeryn stood amidst the wreckage, her eyes scanning the horizon, but she saw nothing. Not the distant peaks where the ice of Thorne's kingdom had once touched the heavens, not the fiery embers of the land she had fought to protect. Only emptiness. Silence. A world broken.

Her heart ached with the weight of her sacrifice. The power that had been unleashed between fire and ice had destroyed everything—everything they had known, everything they had fought for. The very kingdoms that had once been proud, standing tall against the forces of nature, now lay in ruin. And yet, despite the destruction, despite the overwhelming cost of it all, Aeryn knew the hardest part was not the devastation surrounding her. It was the emptiness that remained where Thorne's presence had once been.

Thorne. The man she had loved. The man who had been her equal and her opposite. The man she had given everything for.

His fate had become a shadow she could never quite escape.

The winds shifted, the cold from the north sweeping through her like an unwanted memory. She wrapped her cloak tighter around herself, trying to ignore the chill that seeped deep into her bones. But the cold was not from the wind. It was from within.

"Thorne," she whispered to herself, her voice nearly drowned out by the wind. The last time she had seen him, the storm had consumed them both. The prophecy, the choice, had torn them apart. She had fought to save him, to save them, but now… now, she was left with nothing but the ashes of a broken world and a heart that refused to let go.

Her eyes traced the broken landscape before her—torn earth, scorched fields, shattered buildings, and the scattered remnants of her past. The battle had been won. The storm had passed. But the cost of that victory had left a mark so deep that no amount of time could erase it.

Aeryn had paid the price. A price she was not sure she would ever recover from.

The loss of Thorne felt like a deep wound, one that would never heal. They had defied the prophecy. They had rewritten fate. But at what cost?

A sound broke through her reverie—the distant sound of hooves, a rhythmic pounding that grew louder with each passing second. She turned, her heart lurching in her chest. Could it be? Could someone have survived the devastation?

Could there be hope yet?

As the rider drew closer, Aeryn's breath caught in her throat. A figure rode through the mist, cloaked in shadows, but there was no mistaking the power in the air, the command in the way they moved. Aeryn's pulse quickened.

It was one of her own people.

The rider slowed as they approached, and Aeryn's gaze locked onto the figure beneath the hood. She could see the glint of armor, the unmistakable bearing of someone who had seen battle, who had lived through it and survived. But the face beneath the hood remained hidden.

"Who are you?" Aeryn called out, her voice steady but tinged with suspicion. She knew her people had scattered, had sought refuge in the aftermath of the storm, but she couldn't bring herself to trust anyone—not yet. Not after everything that had happened.

The figure dismounted swiftly, the heavy thud of boots striking the cracked earth reverberating in the silence. The rider removed their hood, revealing a face that Aeryn had not expected.

It was Liora—the trusted lieutenant of Thorne's army, the fierce warrior who had fought alongside them in the battle against the prophecy. Her eyes were dark, haunted by something Aeryn couldn't place. But there was more to her presence than just the shock of seeing a familiar face.

"I thought you lost with the rest," Aeryn said, her voice thick with emotion. She had not expected anyone to return. The battle had taken everyone—except her, it seemed. And now, standing before Liora, she realized that the cost of everything— the cost of victory, of sacrifice—was more than she could have anticipated.

Liora's gaze was steady, unwavering, but her lips were drawn tight, as though the words she had to say were too heavy to bear. "I came to find you," she said, her voice hoarse, as though it had been weeks since she had spoken. "I thought you were dead. We all did."

Aeryn felt a pang of guilt twist inside her. She hadn't realized how much she had left behind—how much she had abandoned in her pursuit of love, of saving them all. She had never thought that she might be the only one left standing.

Liora took a deep breath, her eyes flickering to the ground before meeting Aeryn's gaze again. "There's something you need to know. Something important."

Aeryn felt her heart lurch in her chest. "What is it?"

Liora hesitated for a moment, as if weighing the gravity of the words she was about to speak. "Thorne is alive."

The words hit Aeryn like a wave, crashing into her, pulling her under. She stumbled back a step, her breath catching in her throat. *Alive?*

"Impossible," she whispered, the word barely leaving her lips. "I saw him—he was gone, buried in the storm. The power—it consumed him."

Liora shook her head, her eyes darkening. "It wasn't just his power that was consumed. It was the prophecy. The balance was broken. But the cost… the cost was more than anyone could have anticipated."

Aeryn's mind spun as the weight of Liora's words settled into her. *Thorne was alive.* But at what cost? He had fallen into the storm, into the very chaos they had fought to escape. And now, to learn he was still out there, alive, but possibly changed, was more than Aeryn could process.

"How?" she managed to ask, her voice barely audible.

Liora's expression was grim. "His life force was entwined with the prophecy. He was not meant to survive. But the power of the storm, the merging of fire and ice—it created a rift. He was trapped, lost in between, somewhere between death and life."

Aeryn took a step forward, her body trembling with a mix of fear and hope. "Where is he? Where is Thorne?"

"He's not far," Liora said, her voice softer now, but tinged with sorrow. "But you need to understand, Aeryn. He's not the same. The balance was broken. What's left of him… It's not Thorne. Not in the way you remember."

The air around Aeryn seemed to thicken, and the ground beneath her feet felt unsteady. Her heart twisted in her chest as she absorbed the meaning behind Liora's words. Thorne—her Thorne—was alive, but he was lost, broken, a fragment of the man she had loved.

Aeryn turned her gaze back to the wreckage around them. The kingdom she had fought to save was in ruins, a broken shell of what it had been. She had lost so much already. She had made her sacrifice for love, for them, but now—now, she faced the aftermath. The weight of what was left.

"I need to see him," Aeryn said, her voice strong despite the chaos swirling inside her. "I need to know the truth."

Liora nodded slowly, her gaze softening as she looked at the woman she had once served. "I'll take you to him. But you need to understand, Aeryn. The storm has changed everything. He may not be the man you once knew. And you may not be able to save him this time."

Aeryn took a deep breath, trying to steady her nerves as the weight of her next steps settled over her. She had always believed in love, in the possibility of defying fate. But now, the cost of that love was so much greater than she had ever imagined.

"Take me to him," she said, her voice unwavering despite the uncertainty that churned in her gut. "I'll face whatever it takes. No matter the cost."

Liora nodded and turned her horse, signaling for Aeryn to follow. As they began their journey toward the heart of the ruins—the heart of Thorne's fate—Aeryn couldn't help but wonder if love could truly heal the scars of war. Could it mend the shattered world they had left behind?

Or would the ashes of their past be the only thing that remained?

Aeryn followed Liora through the broken landscape, each step they took bringing them deeper into the heart of a world that had been torn apart. The earth beneath her feet was cracked and scorched, a reflection of the chaos that had erupted between the kingdoms. There was no trace of the vibrant life that had once flourished here, no sign of the hope that had fueled their fight against fate. Now, only desolation remained.

The wind whispered through the ruins, carrying with it the remnants of the battle that had torn their world asunder. Every sound seemed amplified—the crackling of fire in the distance, the unsettling creak of shattered stone as it settled into place, the soft rustling of debris being blown across the broken earth. The silence between Aeryn and Liora was thick with the weight of everything unsaid. The journey ahead felt like a descent into the unknown, and Aeryn could feel the pull of it in her chest.

Thorne...

The name echoed in her mind like a prayer, a desperate cry for something she couldn't quite grasp. He was alive, somewhere ahead of them. But the Thorne she had known, the man who had fought alongside her, loved her with all his heart—was he still the same? Or had the storm taken him from her in ways she couldn't even begin to understand?

Liora's horse moved swiftly, her dark cloak billowing behind her like a shadow, but Aeryn could barely keep up. She had never been a warrior like Liora, never had the strength of the battlefield etched into her muscles the way her old friend did. But she had learned to survive, to push past her fears, especially when it came to Thorne. And right now, fear was all she had. Fear of what she might find. Fear of what Thorne had become. Fear of whether love could ever be enough to heal the scars of the storm that had ravaged them both.

Liora slowed the horse as they approached a crumbling structure—a once-grand building, its walls cracked and half-collapsed, but it still stood. The remnants of magic, of power, lingered in the air. Aeryn felt it the moment they entered, the oppressive weight of something ancient and dangerous, a force she had only ever felt when Thorne was near.

"This is it," Liora said, her voice barely more than a whisper, though the tension in her words was unmistakable. She dismounted gracefully, her boots hitting the earth with a soft thud as she offered Aeryn a hand.

Aeryn hesitated only for a moment, but then, with a deep breath, she took the hand, the cold of Liora's skin startling against the heat of her own. They walked toward the entrance, the air growing thicker with each step. Inside, the remnants of ancient magic pulsed in the walls, the very stones seemingly alive with the energy that had once powered the kingdom. Now, it was a faint echo—a whisper of what had been.

At the center of the room, surrounded by remnants of

the shattered throne, stood Thorne. He was hunched, his figure cloaked in shadows, his back to them. The silence was deafening, and Aeryn's heart stuttered in her chest. She could feel the power radiating from him, but it was different. It wasn't the steady cold she had known. It was something darker, something that had changed him.

"Thorne?" Her voice broke the stillness, soft, tentative, as though she feared that any louder cry would shatter the fragile moment.

He turned slowly, his movements stiff, unnatural. His eyes met hers, and for a fleeting moment, it felt as though time had stopped. His face, once so full of life, now appeared hollow. His skin was pale, too pale, and his eyes—those eyes that had once burned with intensity—were now clouded, distant, as if something of him had been lost. The coldness in his gaze seemed to reach out, wrapping around her heart, threatening to freeze it.

"Aeryn," Thorne whispered, his voice raspy, like someone who had not spoken in too long. "You're here."

Aeryn took a step forward, her heart pounding, her breath shallow. The space between them felt infinite, an unbridgeable chasm of power, loss, and pain. "Thorne…" she whispered again, this time with more strength, the name escaping her lips like a prayer. "You're… alive."

His lips curled into a faint, hollow smile, but it didn't reach his eyes. "I'm alive, but not as I once was."

Aeryn took another step forward, her feet dragging against the heavy air. "What happened to you?" The question felt like a blade lodged in her throat, and she had to swallow hard to push it out. "Where is the Thorne I knew?"

Thorne's gaze shifted downward, his eyes darkening as if

the question had hurt him, had reminded him of everything he had lost. "I am no longer the man you knew, Aeryn. I am the price of our defiance. I am the cost of love. The prophecy has been rewritten, but I… I am a shadow of what I was. A fragment. Trapped between life and death. Between fire and ice."

His words pierced her heart, and Aeryn's hand trembled as she reached out toward him. "No," she whispered, her voice breaking. "You are still the man I loved. You're still *him*. Thorne, please, don't say that. You don't have to carry this burden alone."

But Thorne shook his head slowly, his expression pained. "I *am* alone, Aeryn. I have been for a long time. You were the fire that kept me from drowning in the cold, but I've burned too much. The balance between us—between fire and ice—it was never meant to survive. I was never meant to survive."

Aeryn reached out, her heart desperate to reach him, to feel the warmth of the man she had loved so fiercely. Her fingers brushed against his skin, and the shock of it nearly sent her to her knees. His skin was cold—colder than anything she had ever felt before, like the touch of death itself. She could feel the chill of him seeping into her, into her very bones, and it felt like the last bit of warmth she had once had was being ripped from her.

"No, Thorne," she cried out, her voice cracking. "I won't lose you. I won't."

He closed his eyes, and when he spoke again, his voice was a whisper, as though the words pained him. "You've already lost me, Aeryn. I am not the man you loved. The power between us has destroyed me. And no matter how hard you fight, no matter how much you love me… I cannot come back from this."

Aeryn's heart clenched as she fell to her knees before him, her hands pressing against his icy skin, trying to warm him, trying to *feel* him again. But there was nothing. Nothing that could bridge the chasm that had opened between them.

The silence in the room pressed in on her, suffocating. The storm outside seemed to fade into the background, but the storm within her, within them both, still raged on. She had fought for this. She had fought for him. She had sacrificed everything for the chance to save them both. And now, in this moment, she realized the truth. There was no saving him. There was no coming back from the destruction they had caused.

"Thorne," Aeryn whispered, her voice broken. "You *are* the man I loved. You are still him. And I will never let you go. No matter what it costs."

But as she looked up at him, his eyes meeting hers with a sorrow so deep it threatened to swallow her whole, she knew. He was gone. The man she had loved—the man who had fought by her side, who had shared in her pain and her joy—was lost to the storm. The prophecy had taken him from her, and there was nothing left to do but to accept it.

The cost of their love, of their defiance, had been too great.

And as the room fell into an uneasy silence, the only sound was the quiet hum of the broken world around them, the shattered kingdoms lying in ruins at their feet.

Aeryn's tears fell, the weight of everything pressing down on her. She had lost him. And with him, she had lost the world they had fought for.

But even in the midst of the devastation, there was one thing she knew.

She would rebuild. For the love they had shared. For the man he had been. For the future that was still waiting, even if she had to carry it alone.

And perhaps, just perhaps, their love would survive the ashes.

Eighteen

The Rise of Fire and Ice

The winds had shifted.

Aeryn stood on the edge of the broken citadel, looking out over the land she had once fought so fiercely to protect. Below her, the remnants of the kingdoms sprawled out like a fractured puzzle, a landscape still smoldering in the wake of the final battle. The earth had healed some, but there was no denying the scars left in its wake. Entire cities had been consumed by fire, others swallowed by ice. But it was the silence that stung the most. The land was no longer alive with the energy of its people. It was still—waiting for something, or perhaps, someone.

Her fingers trembled at her sides as she clenched them into fists. She could feel the fire within her, swirling restlessly, yearning for purpose. It had always been her greatest strength and greatest weakness. And now, after everything, it seemed as though the storm inside her had only grown stronger. But it wasn't just her power she felt. It was Thorne's.

She turned her head, her eyes seeking him out.

Thorne stood just a few paces away, his form silhouetted against the twilight sky. The cold radiated from him, an unmistakable chill that seemed to permeate the air around them, but it was different now. The ice that had once been a source of fear and distance between them was now a quiet force, tempered by the fire that had always burned in her. They had been forged together, and now, together, they stood—at the center of everything they had rebuilt.

But the land wasn't the only thing that needed healing.

Their love, once a powerful force against fate itself, was now teetering on the edge. In the aftermath of the storm, Aeryn and Thorne had found themselves at a crossroads. The world had been shattered, and now, they faced the daunting task of rebuilding not just the kingdoms, but their own lives.

"You're thinking too much," Thorne said quietly, his voice carrying the weight of something he had been carrying for far longer than he let on. He turned toward her, his gaze unwavering.

Aeryn swallowed, her eyes locking with his. The silence between them was thick, heavy with unsaid words. She knew what he meant, knew the thoughts that had been swirling in her mind since the battle had ended. The choice before them was more complicated than she had ever imagined.

The storm that had once threatened to destroy them both had been quelled, but it had left something in its wake. Something that neither of them had anticipated. A rift, a tension between them that neither of them could fully address. The balance between fire and ice—their powers—was precarious now. They had fought side by side, but now, as leaders, they were faced with a new question: how would they rule? Could they unite their powers for the greater good, or would they have to remain separate, constantly on the edge of destruction?

Aeryn could feel the weight of that question pressing on her chest, suffocating her with the enormity of the decision. She had been so focused on love, on the sacrifice they had made, that she had ignored the complexities of what came after. The kingdoms were fragile. The people were fragile. And she and Thorne… were fragile.

"I don't know what to do, Thorne," she whispered, her voice barely audible over the howling winds. "I thought I had all the answers, but now… everything feels uncertain. We're not the same. I'm not the same."

He stepped closer to her, the icy chill of his presence radiating around them, but this time, it didn't feel cold. It was grounding, anchoring her in the moment. He reached out, his hand brushing against hers, and for a fleeting moment, their powers seemed to merge, fire and ice intertwining in a gentle dance that felt like the calm before the storm.

"I know," Thorne said softly, his voice laced with understanding. "I feel it too. We're both different now. But that doesn't mean we can't move forward."

Aeryn closed her eyes, taking a deep breath as the weight of their shared responsibility settled into her bones. There was so much at stake. The kingdoms needed leadership—strong leadership—but the strength they needed wasn't just in their individual powers. It was in their ability to navigate the delicate balance between them, to find a way to merge fire and ice without destroying everything they had rebuilt.

"I've been thinking about it too much," Aeryn admitted, finally opening her eyes to meet his gaze. "I've been trying to force the pieces together, thinking that if we just… if we just pushed through, it would be enough. But it's not. We can't keep pretending we're the same as we were before."

Thorne nodded, his jaw tightening as though he was fighting something inside himself. "We're not the same. And I don't want us to be. But that doesn't mean we're not enough. Together."

Together.

The word echoed between them, heavy with meaning. Aeryn knew what it meant. They had always been stronger together. Their love had been a force—fire and ice, the perfect balance. But now, after everything they had been through, the balance felt more fragile than ever before.

"I want to be enough," Aeryn said, her voice soft but firm. "For you. For them. But I don't know if we can keep doing this the same way. I don't know if we can keep fighting the same fight. We can't keep ruling with fire and ice separated. If we do that, we'll keep destroying what we're trying to rebuild."

Thorne's gaze softened, the coldness in his eyes fading as he stepped closer to her, his presence surrounding her with warmth. He took her hand in his, the warmth of his skin somehow making the chill inside her seem less daunting. "We're not just fire and ice, Aeryn. We're more. Together, we create something stronger—something new."

Aeryn looked up at him, her heart pounding in her chest. She could feel the weight of his words, the truth of them settling in her bones. They couldn't keep fighting the same fight. They couldn't keep holding on to the past. They had to create something new.

But the question remained: *Could they?*

The silence between them stretched, filled with the weight of their decision. Aeryn could hear the soft rhythm of her heart, and for the first time in what felt like forever, she was at peace. Not because everything was right—far from it—but because she knew that together, they could face whatever came next. The balance would be precarious, yes. But they would find a way to walk the razor's edge.

"We have to unite," Aeryn said finally, her voice steady despite the fear that lingered in the back of her mind. "We have to bring our powers together, or everything we've fought for will be for nothing."

Thorne nodded slowly, his eyes filled with a quiet resolve. "Then we unite. And we rebuild. Not just the kingdoms, but ourselves. We start over. Together."

For a moment, Aeryn allowed herself to believe it. The weight of the decision, the uncertainty of their future, was still there, but in that moment, it felt like something she could carry. Something they could carry together.

But as she turned to face the kingdom, as she looked out at the remains of a broken world, she felt a shift in the air— something new, something dark. The winds had shifted again, but this time, it wasn't the calm before the storm. It was the whisper of a new danger, a shadow that had begun to rise from the ashes.

The balance between fire and ice had never been so fragile. And as Aeryn and Thorne took their first steps toward rebuilding their world, they both knew that the future was uncertain. But one thing was clear: the world had changed, and so had they. Their love was no longer just a force that could destroy—it was the foundation upon which a new world would rise.

But with every new beginning, there was always the shadow

of something more. Something that would test them in ways they couldn't yet imagine.

And as the night deepened, Aeryn felt it. The darkness that had begun to stir, the threat that was lurking just beyond the horizon.

The storm was not over. It was only just beginning.

Aeryn stood still, her eyes fixed on the horizon, where the faintest shadow seemed to shift in the twilight. The wind had picked up again, but it was different this time—colder, sharper. She could feel it in the pit of her stomach, a sense of unease that seemed to pulse through the very air, like the calm before a storm. The storm, yes, but not the one they had already fought. This one was something else.

Thorne, still by her side, sensed it too. She could feel his presence beside her—his strength, the icy power that had always been part of him, now tempered by the fire they had shared. He was silent, but she didn't need words. His body had stiffened, his gaze locked on the same distant shadow that had drawn her own attention.

"What is it?" she whispered, her voice trembling not from fear but from the awareness of something old and dangerous stirring in the air around them.

Thorne didn't answer immediately. He shifted slightly, his ice-blue eyes narrowing. His hand, once gentle in its touch, tightened on hers, and for the first time in what felt like an eternity, Aeryn realized how much they were both still tethered to their past. To their shared destiny.

"I don't know," he said finally, his voice rough. "But I feel it too."

The wind howled around them, the remnants of their

fractured world now swept into the gusts, the air heavy with the scent of ash and rain. The once grand citadel behind them—the symbol of their shared triumph—seemed so distant, so insignificant now. It was not just the land that had been torn apart. It was the very fabric of everything they had fought to rebuild. What they had started now felt fragile, incomplete.

"Who's there?" Aeryn called out, her voice sharper now, cutting through the wind. She wasn't sure if it was a question or a challenge, but she couldn't keep the fear from creeping into her chest.

A figure appeared on the horizon, cloaked in shadows. At first, it was little more than a silhouette against the dimming sky, but the figure was moving toward them with purpose, unhurried, almost casual. It was a woman—Aeryn could tell from the way she moved, the fluid grace in her steps, though she could not make out any further details.

"She's coming for us," Thorne muttered under his breath, his voice like ice, a familiar chill of tension tightening in his words. He stepped closer to Aeryn, his arm brushing against hers, but it wasn't comfort she felt in that touch—it was the old sense of dread, the one they had never fully shaken, the one that still lurked at the edges of their shared power.

The woman stopped a few paces away, standing just beyond the reach of their combined powers. Her eyes were dark, her gaze piercing, and Aeryn could feel an unsettling power radiating from her—a force as ancient and deep as the earth itself. It wasn't the raw energy of fire or ice; this was something else, something older, something more insidious.

"Who are you?" Aeryn demanded, her voice steady now, despite the unease creeping up her spine.

The woman smiled, a cold, knowing smile. "I am someone

who knows what you've become. And what you have yet to face."

Aeryn's heart skipped a beat. The woman's words hung in the air like an omen, as if they were part of a prophecy yet to be fulfilled. She didn't like the sound of it, didn't trust the certainty in the woman's voice.

"Speak plainly," Thorne said, his tone flat, controlled, but there was an edge to it that Aeryn recognized—his power was shifting, the ice within him sharpening, as if he too could feel the danger in the air.

The woman tilted her head slightly, studying them both with eyes that seemed to see through them. "You've rebuilt what's broken, but it's fragile. Do you think the world can survive the union of fire and ice? You've changed the course of history, yes, but you've also set something in motion you cannot stop."

Aeryn's heart pounded in her chest. "What do you mean? What's coming?"

The woman laughed softly, the sound like ice cracking in the dead of winter. "What you've done—what you've *created*—has caused ripples, Aeryn. Ripples that will pull everything into the storm. Your love is the catalyst for something much darker than you realize. The balance of fire and ice… it can't exist for long. There must be destruction before rebirth. That is the way of this world."

Aeryn's mind raced as the woman's words settled into her chest like stones. She turned to Thorne, his face pale, his eyes narrowing with understanding, and a sense of dread blossomed in her gut. What had they *really* done? Had they just exchanged one form of destruction for another?

The woman stepped closer, her movements smooth, fluid, like a predator circling its prey. "The kingdoms may be broken, but there are others who see your bond as a threat. A *gift* that must be destroyed before it spreads."

Aeryn's eyes widened. "Who would seek to destroy what we've rebuilt?"

The woman's smile deepened, her gaze flickering between Aeryn and Thorne. "The ones who remain in the shadows, watching. They are the ones who know the true power of what you've become. They will come for you, for your love, for your strength. The rise of fire and ice has already begun. You must decide now whether you will rule separately or let your powers combine and risk everything."

Aeryn felt her heart skip a beat. The balance was already precarious—if they allowed their powers to merge completely, what would happen? They had always fought together, side by side, but could they afford to become one? Could they afford to take the risk of combining their strengths and opening the door to something even greater than what they had already unleashed?

Thorne turned to her, his icy gaze meeting hers. "We've already crossed that line, Aeryn," he said quietly. "We've united once before, in the storm. We can't go back now."

But Aeryn wasn't so sure. She could feel the fire inside her, restless, yearning for more, but it was tempered by the coldness that Thorne had always carried, and now, in the aftermath, that coldness felt like an anchor, pulling them both down into the depths of something they might not be able to escape.

The woman in front of them raised her hand, as though sensing the conflict between them. "The choice is yours," she said, her voice a whisper, yet it rang loud in the silence between them. "You can stand together, united, but the cost will be greater than you realize. Or you can separate, keep your powers in check, and rule the remnants of this broken world in the shadows of your former selves."

The wind shifted again, colder, sharper, and Aeryn could feel the pressure building inside her, inside Thorne. Their powers were calling to each other, but so was the weight of the world pressing down on them. The question that had always lingered—the question of their union, of their love—was now more urgent than ever.

The woman turned away, her cloak billowing around her like smoke, and she walked back into the shadows, her words echoing in the growing silence. "Remember, the storm has only begun. Choose wisely."

Aeryn stood frozen in place, the weight of her decision bearing down on her like a collapsing mountain. She turned to Thorne, their eyes locking, both of them filled with a shared understanding that had not been there before. The world was fractured, the kingdoms shattered. They had been given a chance to rebuild, but the price of their love—of their bond— had always been higher than either of them had realized.

"What do we do now?" Aeryn asked, her voice barely above a whisper.

Thorne's hand reached for hers, his grip cold but steady. "We face it. Together. We decide our future. No matter the cost."

The wind howled again, but this time, it didn't feel like an omen. It felt like a promise.

And Aeryn knew, deep in her bones, that the storm had only just begun.

Nineteen

The Flames of Destiny

The air was thick with tension as Aeryn stood at the precipice, her eyes scanning the horizon, watching the faint traces of the coming storm darken the sky. The wind whipped through her hair, and she could feel the heat rising inside her—heat that she had long since come to accept, a fire that had always been a part of her. But today, it felt different. The air around her was charged, electric, as though the very atmosphere was holding its breath, waiting for something to happen.

Beside her, Thorne's presence was a steadying force, but even he, usually so calm and controlled, seemed to be vibrating with the same tension she felt deep within herself. His ice-blue eyes were narrowed, his jaw tight, as though he was wrestling with the same uneasy sensation. The winds that had once been familiar, that had once seemed like a shield for his power, now felt like they were turning against them both.

"Aeryn," Thorne's voice was low, his tone rough with barely-contained emotion. "Something's wrong. I can feel it. The storm—it's not just the weather. It's more than that."

Aeryn turned to him, her heart sinking as she saw the concern in his eyes. He had always been able to sense things, to feel the shifts in the world around them. But now, his power was reacting to something neither of them could quite understand. The battle they had fought, the war they had won, was supposed to have brought peace—but now, it felt as if they were on the cusp of something far more dangerous.

"I feel it too," she admitted, her voice barely a whisper, though her heart pounded in her chest. "But what is it? What could be worse than what we've already faced?"

Thorne's hand brushed against hers, his icy touch familiar and grounding. But even that didn't soothe the unease spiraling within her. She had never been more acutely aware of the fragility of everything they had fought for. The love they shared—the fire and ice that had always existed between them—had been the force that had brought them this far. But now, as they stood at the edge of a world they had rebuilt, they were about to face something that could tear it all apart.

The ground beneath them trembled, a low rumble that vibrated through the soles of Aeryn's boots, and the sky above them darkened even further, as if the heavens themselves were preparing for the coming battle. The air felt heavy, suffocating. It was as though the world was holding its breath, waiting for something to break.

Thorne stepped forward, his gaze unwavering, his eyes scanning the horizon. "There's something in the air, Aeryn. A new force is rising."

Aeryn's heart skipped a beat as she followed his gaze, her

senses on high alert. In the distance, something was moving—shadows, flickers of movement just beyond the edge of the ruins. She couldn't make out the shape, but the feeling of malevolence was palpable, a dark force that was drawing nearer with every passing second.

"I don't know what it is," Aeryn murmured, her voice tense, "but I can feel it too. Whatever it is, it's not natural."

Thorne turned toward her, his expression hardening. "We need to prepare. Whatever is coming—it's going to test us. It's going to test everything we've fought for."

Aeryn nodded, her chest tightening. They had already sacrificed so much. They had defied fate itself, overcome insurmountable odds to bring peace to the kingdoms. But now, the very peace they had fought for was under threat again. And this time, the battle would not be just about the kingdoms or the prophecy. It would be about their love, their bond, and whether it was strong enough to withstand whatever this new force was.

"We've fought together before," Aeryn said, her voice steady despite the fear curling in her gut. "We can do it again. We *have* to."

Thorne reached for her, his icy fingers brushing against her skin, sending a shiver through her body. The fire inside her flared in response, a flicker of heat igniting at the base of her spine. She could feel their power—*their* power—pulsing between them, a force that had once been their strength and their salvation. But now, it felt different. Stronger. More dangerous.

"We'll face this together, Aeryn," Thorne said quietly, his voice thick with emotion. "But I need you to promise me something."

Aeryn looked up at him, her heart in her throat. "What?"

His eyes softened, the coldness that had always been part of him now tempered by the warmth of his love for her. "No matter what happens, no matter what we face… don't lose yourself. Don't lose *us*."

Aeryn's breath caught in her throat. The weight of his words sank deep into her chest. She had never thought about it—never truly allowed herself to consider the cost of what their love had done, of what it had become. It had always been a force, an undeniable power that had brought them together, that had driven them forward. But now, with everything at stake, the very foundation of their love was being tested.

"I won't," she whispered, her voice firm with the promise of it. She took his hand in hers, squeezing it tightly. "We'll face this together. Whatever comes."

They stood together, their powers a quiet storm between them, and in that moment, Aeryn knew that they would fight for each other, for their love, no matter the cost. The world might have been shattered, the balance between fire and ice fragile, but their love was a constant—something that could survive even the darkest of storms.

The shadow in the distance drew closer, the air heavy with the scent of ozone and burning embers. The figure emerged from the darkness, moving with a slow, deliberate grace, the ground beneath her feet seeming to tremble in response to her presence. Aeryn's pulse quickened as the woman stepped into the light, revealing her form.

The woman was cloaked in dark robes, her features obscured by a hood, but the power radiating from her was undeniable. Aeryn could feel it—the same energy that had once belonged to the storm they had fought to survive. But this was different.

This was darker.

The woman's eyes glowed faintly, a cold, unnatural light that sent a chill down Aeryn's spine. "So, the fire and ice remain," the woman said, her voice a low, menacing whisper that seemed to seep into the air like poison. "Together, once more. How… *romantic*."

Aeryn's heart skipped a beat, but she didn't flinch. "Who are you?" she demanded, her voice steady despite the overwhelming force of the woman's presence. "What do you want?"

The woman tilted her head, a wicked smile curling on her lips. "What I want… is to see you both burn."

Thorne stepped forward, his hand tightening around the hilt of his sword, his icy power flickering in the air around him. "You think you can threaten us?" His voice was cold, but Aeryn could sense the tension in it—the unease that came from facing an enemy unlike any they had fought before.

"Oh, I don't think," the woman said, her voice thick with amusement. "I *know*. You've only seen a fraction of what's coming. Your love, your bond, it's the only thing standing in the way of what I'm about to bring."

Aeryn's heart raced, the warning in the woman's voice sending a shiver through her. She could feel the weight of it, the power that seemed to build in the air around them, a storm that was rising once more—but this time, it wasn't just the weather. It was something far more dangerous. Something that would tear apart the fragile peace they had fought so hard to create.

"What do you want?" Aeryn asked again, her voice rising with a sense of urgency.

The woman's smile widened. "I want to see the end of the fire and ice. I want to see the balance break completely. And when it does, the world will be mine to control."

Thorne's eyes narrowed, his grip tightening. Aeryn felt the coldness of his power surge in response, but there was a flicker of doubt in him—a hesitation she hadn't seen before. Was he truly afraid? Or was it something else?

"Your fight is with me," Aeryn said, stepping forward, her fire flaring in response to the woman's dark power. "Leave him out of this."

The woman's laugh was sharp, cutting through the tension like a blade. "Oh, I think not, little firebird. You *are* the key. You and your love. That is what will destroy you both."

Aeryn's heart thundered in her chest. The world they had fought for—*their* world—was at risk once again. But this time, there was no going back. The balance between them, between fire and ice, was fragile. They had already broken the rules of fate once before. But could they do it again?

And more importantly—could they survive what was about to come?

The woman raised her hands, and the air around them began to pulse with power. Aeryn felt it in her bones, the shift, the change, the storm that was about to break.

Thorne's grip on her hand tightened. "Aeryn…" he whispered.

"I'm with you," she said, her voice unwavering.

And together, they faced the storm once more—fire and ice, love and destiny, standing strong against the darkness that threatened to tear them apart.

The world was about to burn. And they would either rise from the ashes—or be consumed by them.

The air crackled with energy, a tension so thick it was almost suffocating. The woman before them, cloaked in shadow, was no longer just a figure of menace. She was the embodiment of the storm that had been gathering, a dark force that had risen from the ashes of their once fractured world. Her eyes glowed faintly, like the embers of a dying fire, and Aeryn could feel the weight of her gaze bearing down on her, like the pressure of an impending avalanche.

Thorne's grip tightened around Aeryn's hand, his ice-cold touch sending a jolt of unease through her. She could feel the icy storm within him rising, his power swirling dangerously, but there was something different in the air now—a sense of finality. This wasn't just a battle. This was the moment where everything they had fought for would either be destroyed or forever changed.

The woman lifted her hands, and the ground beneath them trembled, as if answering her call. A low, rumbling sound filled the air, like thunder rolling across the sky. But this wasn't the sound of a natural storm. This was something darker, something more ancient. Aeryn's heart beat faster as she stepped forward, her feet steady despite the fear gripping her chest.

"Enough games," Aeryn said, her voice cutting through the tension. She could feel the fire in her veins, the flames flickering at the edges of her control. "Tell us who you are."

The woman smiled, a cruel twist of her lips that sent a chill down Aeryn's spine. "I am the one who has watched your love grow—watched you both, fire and ice, tear the world apart and try to rebuild it in your own image. But it's time to pay the price for your defiance. Your love is the key to unlocking the true power of this world, and I will be the one to wield it."

Aeryn's pulse quickened. *She knows us,* she thought, her mind racing. The woman wasn't just a stranger. She knew what they were—what they had become. She knew their bond, their powers. She knew everything.

The winds around them began to pick up, swirling faster, hotter, colder—fire and ice, a perfect storm building. The woman's hands were raised high, and Aeryn could feel the ground beneath her shifting. There was something dark within this place—something ancient and powerful, buried deep beneath the earth. It was as though the very world was rejecting them, the air heavy with the force of what was about to unfold.

Thorne took a step forward, his voice like ice itself, cold and unyielding. "You're playing with forces you don't understand."

The woman's eyes gleamed, her smile widening. "Oh, I understand them perfectly. And now, I will use them to bring your kingdoms to their knees."

She extended her arms, and the ground seemed to crack open beneath them, sending a shockwave through the earth. Aeryn stumbled back, her heart pounding in her chest. A wave of energy surged through the air—blinding, suffocating, a power so pure that it made her head spin. Her body flared with heat, the fire within her roaring in response to the immense pressure bearing down on her.

"We cannot let this happen," Aeryn said, her voice trembling with a mixture of fear and defiance. Her eyes met Thorne's, and in that moment, everything else faded away. There was only him. Only their love. Only the unbreakable bond that had kept them alive through every battle, every sacrifice.

"Together," Thorne whispered, his breath steady despite the chaos that surrounded them. "We'll stop her. *Together.*"

Aeryn nodded, her heart swelling with the truth of his words.

She had always known they were stronger together, but now, in this moment, it felt like they were the only ones who could stop the storm that was rising—both inside them and in the world around them.

Thorne raised his hand, and the air around them grew colder, his ice powers swirling in a vortex of raw energy. The ground beneath them froze, cracks running through the earth like veins of lightning. Aeryn felt the fire within her flare, her flames reacting to the coldness of his power, the two forces entwining in a delicate balance.

The woman's laugh echoed through the air, cruel and sharp. "You think you can stop me? You think your love can save you?"

Aeryn's heart burned with fury. "Our love is stronger than anything you can throw at us."

With a fierce cry, Aeryn released the fire inside her, the flames shooting out in a brilliant burst of light. The heat surged, crackling through the air like a storm unleashed. Thorne's ice surged in response, the cold wrapping around the fire, creating a whirlwind of power—a storm of their own making.

The woman raised her arms higher, and the ground beneath them began to shake. "You cannot hold back the storm forever," she sneered. "You will burn, or you will freeze. Either way, you will be consumed."

But Aeryn didn't flinch. She didn't hesitate. She had fought too long, lost too much, to give up now. She and Thorne had always known their love came at a cost, but they had also known that together, they could face anything.

With a fierce cry, she released the full force of her flames, the fire surging from her in a wave of heat that clashed violently against Thorne's ice. The two forces collided with such intensity that the very air around them seemed to burn and freeze all at once.

The ground trembled beneath them as the woman's laughter grew louder, more manic. She seemed to feed off their struggle, her energy building with every flicker of their power. But Aeryn could feel it now—the shift. The crack in the woman's control. The chaos was a part of her, yes, but it was also consuming her. The woman's power was turning against her, the balance of fire and ice threatening to unravel everything she had built.

"We're stronger than you," Aeryn shouted, her voice carrying over the battle. "You can't control us. You can't control our love."

The woman's eyes flashed with rage. "You think you've won? You think this is over?"

But Aeryn didn't answer. Instead, she focused all of her energy on the fire inside her, pushing past the exhaustion, past the fear. This time, the flames burned brighter, hotter. They began to consume the darkness that surrounded them, eating away at the shadows the woman had summoned.

Thorne's voice rang out beside her, calm and determined. "Aeryn, together."

Aeryn looked to him, and in his eyes, she saw the truth. They were no longer just fire and ice. They were something more—something stronger. Together, they could overcome anything.

With one final push, Aeryn and Thorne released their combined power, the fire and ice merging into a single force that blasted forward like a tidal wave. The woman's scream echoed through the air as the energy they unleashed enveloped her, burning away the darkness that had held her together. The shadows writhed, shrinking in the face of their combined might, and then, with a deafening crack, the woman's form shattered like glass, her power dissolving into the wind.

For a moment, there was only silence. The storm raged around them, but it was no longer a threat. It was just the wind, the remnants of the battle they had won. Aeryn and Thorne stood side by side, their bodies shaking with the aftermath of their power, but they were alive. Together.

Aeryn looked at Thorne, her chest heaving with the weight of what they had just done. "We did it," she said, her voice rough with emotion.

Thorne reached for her, his hand warm despite the chill that still lingered in the air. "We did," he said softly. "And we'll keep doing it. Together."

For the first time since the storm had begun, Aeryn allowed herself to believe it. They had faced the darkness. They had fought for their love, for their world. And now, as the storm began to die down, as the world began to heal, she realized something.

Their love was not just the key to saving the world—it was the force that would rebuild it, one step at a time. No matter the cost. No matter what came next.

Together, they would face it. And together, they would rise.

Twenty

The Final Embrace

The sky above them was as dark as a bruise, the storm that had been churning in the distance now fully upon them. Aeryn could feel the electricity in the air, the sense of impending doom crackling through her veins. The wind howled like a thousand voices in pain, swirling around them in a frenzy that seemed to mirror the chaos in her heart.

She stood at the edge of the cliff, the land below her a crumbling wasteland. The earth, scarred by fire and ice, was still reeling from the destruction they had wrought, and the very air felt thick with the weight of everything they had lost. But it was also filled with something else—a sense of finality, a sense that whatever came next would be the last battle. The last test.

Aeryn could feel the fire within her, the heat of it burning hot, swirling around her like a protective shield, but she also felt the cold. The chill that emanated from Thorne, still standing beside her, his presence a grounding force even in the face of everything that was about to unfold. His icy power had always been a part of him, a part of their bond, but now, it was more than that. It was *them*—fire and ice, two forces that had shaped not just their love, but their destiny.

"Are you ready?" Thorne asked, his voice a low whisper against the roar of the wind. His hand brushed against hers, and for a brief moment, the warmth of his touch cut through the cold that surrounded them. But the moment passed, and the chill returned, a reminder of the impossible choice before them.

Aeryn turned her head to look at him. His face was as unreadable as it had always been, but in his eyes, she saw something deeper—something that mirrored the turmoil inside her. The man she had loved, the man who had stood by her side through every trial, every battle, was still here. But the world they had fought to rebuild was now hanging by a thread.

"We don't have a choice," Aeryn replied, her voice steady despite the storm in her chest. "Whatever happens now, we face it together. There is no turning back."

Thorne nodded, his eyes meeting hers with a quiet understanding. The silence between them spoke volumes, the weight of everything they had been through hanging in the air like a storm cloud waiting to break.

But just as she felt the first stirrings of peace, the earth beneath their feet trembled. Aeryn's heart skipped a beat, her body bracing for whatever came next. She had felt this before—the ground shifting, the earth groaning beneath the strain of their love, of their combined powers. But this time, it felt different. It felt like something had been unleashed that couldn't be controlled.

From the shadows, a figure emerged, stepping out from the chaos, her presence so cold that it chilled the air around them. The woman—the one who had come to them before, the one who had spoken of their love as a curse—was here again, her dark eyes gleaming with malevolent power.

"You," Aeryn whispered, the word slipping from her lips like a curse. "What do you want now?"

The woman's smile was slow, cruel. "You've come so far, haven't you? You've fought so hard for what you have now. But the question remains—will you survive this final test?"

Thorne stepped forward, his body tense, his powers crackling with cold energy. "We've already faced the darkness, and we've won. What makes you think this time will be any different?"

The woman's laugh was sharp, cutting through the tension between them. "You've won battles, yes. But this is the war. The war for the future of your world. And in the end, the flames of destiny must burn brighter than ice. One of you will fall, and the other will carry the burden. That is the price of defying fate."

Aeryn's heart clenched at her words, but she didn't let the fear rise. They had faced the darkness before. They had rewritten their fate, defied the prophecy, and yet, here they stood, still alive, still fighting for the future. Their love was not a curse—it was their strength. Together, they were unstoppable.

"We'll face whatever comes," Aeryn said, her voice firm. "And together, we will win. No matter the cost."

The woman's eyes narrowed, and the air around them shifted. The temperature dropped, a sharp, biting cold that seemed to seep into their bones. The wind howled, and Aeryn could feel the power building—something ancient, something dangerous. The world around them seemed to hold its breath, as if waiting for the moment that would define everything.

Thorne's voice was low, but there was a sharp edge to it now. "Whatever happens, Aeryn, we face this together. We've always faced it together."

Aeryn turned to him, her heart swelling with love and fear in equal measure. He was right. They had always been stronger together, and that strength was what had carried them through everything. No matter what the woman said, no matter what fate had in store, their love would be the key to saving them.

"I'm with you," Aeryn said, her voice fierce, her grip tightening on his hand. "Always."

The woman's laugh cut through the air, filled with malice. "You think your love will save you? It will be your downfall."

The ground beneath them cracked, the air thick with the power that surged between fire and ice. Aeryn felt the flames inside her surge, the heat building until it was almost unbearable. At the same time, she could feel the coldness of Thorne's power, pulling at her, pushing against her fire, as if testing their bond.

The woman raised her hands, and the world around them seemed to bend, the sky darkening further, the winds growing colder. "This is it. The final test. Will you survive the flames of destiny, or will you burn in the cold of fate?"

Aeryn and Thorne exchanged a look, a silent understanding passing between them. They had come this far, defied everything that had been thrown their way. They would not back down now.

With a cry, Aeryn released her power, the flames surging from her in a wave of heat that lit up the sky. Thorne followed suit, his icy powers pushing against the fire, creating a storm of raw energy that crackled between them. Their combined strength was enough to shake the very earth beneath their feet.

But the woman's power was just as great. She was the embodiment of the storm, the embodiment of everything they had feared. She summoned her own power, a dark energy that twisted the air around them, pulling at the earth, at the very fabric of the world they had tried so desperately to rebuild.

The forces collided—fire and ice, darkness and light—and the earth seemed to shudder under the weight of it all. The wind howled, and for a moment, Aeryn felt as though everything around her was being torn apart. The pain of it—of their love, of their sacrifice—was almost too much to bear.

But then, in the heart of the storm, Aeryn felt something shift. It was the connection between them, the love they had fought for, the love that had always been the key to their survival. It wasn't just fire and ice. It was *them*. Together, they were more than the sum of their parts. Their love was the force that could change everything.

With a final, desperate cry, Aeryn and Thorne focused all of their power into one singular moment. The fire flared, the ice surged, and for an instant, the world seemed to stop. The storm, the darkness, the woman—all of it was consumed by the explosion of energy that erupted from them. The force of their love, their combined power, tore through the very fabric of the world, reshaping it in the blink of an eye.

The world went silent.

Aeryn's chest heaved as she collapsed into Thorne's arms, her body trembling with exhaustion, but there was something else now. Peace. The storm had passed. The darkness was gone.

She looked up at him, her heart swelling with love and relief. "We did it," she whispered.

Thorne's arms tightened around her, and for the first time, she saw a softness in his eyes that had been absent before. "Together."

And in that moment, Aeryn knew. They had faced the final test. They had rewritten their fate, not with fire or ice, but with their love. And no matter the cost, no matter the sacrifices, they had won.

The world had been saved—not by force, not by power—but by the strength of their love.

And as they stood there, together, at the end of everything, Aeryn realized that their love was the only thing that truly mattered. It was the key to saving their world. It was the heart of fire and ice.

And it would burn forever.

The wind had stilled. The storm that had raged around them, tearing at the very fabric of their world, had finally ceased. In its place was a haunting, perfect silence that felt more real than anything Aeryn had ever known. The air was heavy, but there was no longer the suffocating weight of impending destruction. Instead, there was only the coolness of the night and the warmth of Thorne's embrace.

Aeryn's eyes fluttered open, her breath slow and deep as she inhaled the calm air. Her body ached, every muscle protesting the immense strain of their final battle, but the exhaustion was tempered by a quiet peace. She felt Thorne's presence, strong and unwavering, still holding her in his arms, but she didn't need to look up to know that the world had changed.

The force of their love had cut through the storm, and now,

they stood on the other side. Together.

Thorne's hand rested on the small of her back, his touch still cold, yet somehow comforting. She felt the quiet rhythm of his heartbeat, steady beneath her ear. She could feel his power still flickering—like the last embers of a fire, the ice within him still glowing with the remnants of their combined strength.

Aeryn swallowed, her throat dry as she lifted her head, her eyes meeting his.

"Is it over?" she whispered, her voice hoarse from the battle and the rawness of everything they had been through.

Thorne didn't answer immediately. His gaze shifted, searching the horizon, where the dark clouds had finally parted, revealing the first signs of dawn. The pale light of the new day illuminated the broken world below them, the ruins of the kingdoms they had rebuilt—shattered, yes, but not defeated. The damage was done, but there was hope now. A quiet hope that would take time to grow, but it was there.

"I think it is," Thorne said softly, his voice carrying an edge of disbelief, as though he couldn't quite comprehend what had just happened. "We've crossed the threshold, Aeryn. Together. We faced the final test."

Aeryn nodded, her eyes closing briefly as the weight of his words sank in. She had never imagined this moment, never truly believed it could come. That after everything, after the destruction, the battles, the sacrifices, they would still stand. Still be here. Together.

"I can't believe it's finally over," Aeryn said, her voice barely more than a whisper. "We did it."

Thorne's lips curled into a faint, bittersweet smile. "We did. But at what cost?"

Aeryn looked up at him then, her eyes searching his face,

tracing the familiar lines of his features, the ones she had come to memorize through countless trials and battles. There were shadows in his eyes now—shadows of the past, of the struggle they had endured, of the love they had fought for. And yet, in the midst of it all, there was something else. Something that gave her the strength to believe, even now, that their future would be brighter.

"The cost is always high," Aeryn said softly, her hand lifting to touch his cheek, feeling the icy chill of his skin beneath her fingers. "But it was worth it. We were worth it."

Thorne's gaze softened, his expression almost tender. He reached up, his own hand brushing against her hair, pushing a stray lock of damp hair from her face. "I don't know what I'd have done without you, Aeryn. I never thought we would make it this far."

Aeryn smiled then, the corners of her lips lifting despite the exhaustion in her bones. "You're not getting rid of me that easily, Thorne. You and I, we're in this together, for better or worse."

Thorne chuckled softly, a rare, genuine laugh that warmed her heart. He pressed his forehead against hers, closing his eyes for a moment as if savoring the peace, the moment of quiet that had settled between them. "For better or worse, indeed."

The first rays of sunlight began to break over the horizon, casting a golden glow over the devastated land. Aeryn felt the warmth of it, the promise of a new day. The storm had passed. The destruction had been fierce, and the scars would remain, but there was something different now. The world was not the same, but it was not beyond saving.

Together, they had fought. Together, they had triumphed.

And now, together, they would rebuild.

Aeryn stepped back, pulling away from Thorne, and for a moment, they stood there, looking at the broken world before them. There was no denying that the road ahead would be long and difficult. The damage was too great to be undone overnight. But the power of their love—the strength they had found in each other—was something that would endure. They had rewritten their destiny, and now, it was theirs to shape.

Thorne's voice broke the silence, low and steady. "What happens now, Aeryn?"

Aeryn turned to him, meeting his gaze with a fierce determination in her eyes. "Now, we rebuild. We make sure what we fought for wasn't in vain. And we do it together, one step at a time."

Thorne's lips curved into a smile, though it was filled with something deeper than just relief. It was a promise—a promise that no matter the obstacles ahead, no matter the scars left behind, they would face it together.

"I'm with you," he said, his voice strong, steady. "Always."

Aeryn felt the truth of his words settle deep in her heart. Together. They would face the future, side by side, fire and ice, bound by the love that had always defined them.

As the sun rose higher in the sky, casting light on the shattered kingdoms, Aeryn and Thorne stood together, ready to face whatever the future held. The final test had been passed. The world was scarred, yes, but it was not lost.

And as long as they were together, there was nothing they couldn't rebuild.

The flames of destiny had tested them. But their love had survived, and it would burn brighter than ever before.

The world would never be the same—but neither would they.

www.ingramcontent.com/pod-product-compliance
Lightning Source LLC
LaVergne TN
LVHW041311200726
843509LV00009B/455